CONVERSATIONAL COMMENTARY ON

2 TIMOTHY

*The Good Fight
for a Faithful Finish*

BY MICHELLE MYERS

S W H W
SHE WORKS HIS WAY

Conversational Commentary on 2 Timothy
The Good Fight for a Faithful Finish

©2023 Myers Cross Training
His Way Resources, Inc.
Design + Layout ©2023 Erica Zoller Creative, LLC

ISBN 978-1-7345281-9-0

CONTENTS

Acknowledgments

My Bible margins are filled with notes I've written over the years -- a combination of sermons heard and books read, lecture notes during seminary, insights from countless discipleship groups, retreats and conferences, as well as my own personal study. To all who have used your gifts as stewards of God's grace, I am forever grateful for your investment in my life and the lives of many others.

I also can't miss the opportunity to extend a special thank you to Mark + Pat Cooper. While James and I were super young in marriage and ministry, you "Timothy'd" us from the moment we met. Three kids, two moves and over a decade later, you're still doing it. On behalf of everyone you've mentored throughout the years, thank you for investing in us, praying for us and loving us so well. We are so grateful to God for you!

- Michelle Myers

CONVERSATIONAL COMMENTARY ON 2 TIMOTHY:

Introducing Conversational Commentary

Some of my favorite moments take place in church or a living room with other women gathered around an open Bible. It's during those moments when I see for myself that God's Word is living and active *(Hebrews 4:12)*, when I'm taught by older women and am able to teach younger women, and when that teaching isn't merely done with words but is coupled with an example *(Titus 2:1-5)*.

So when God first began stirring this series in my heart, I wondered if it would be possible to create a gospel-centered conversation that would take place inside gospel community -- not just writing content. Because this world is not lacking in good -- *yes, even gospel-centered* -- information. We also have more distribution channels to provide the information to more people in ways that are quick, cost-efficient, and convenient to access. I'm grateful for these outlets. Any place the gospel can be proclaimed is reason to rejoice. But the good information and great distribution are not enough on their own. As believers, we're *all* called to be disciples who make disciples -- and that cannot be automated and distributed, delegated to some, or designed for the masses.

So that's where the idea of writing conversational commentary began. God's Word is God speaking to us, we get to continue the conversation He started in the commentary, and the corresponding questions enable you to build discipleship relationships with women you know.

WHAT TO EXPECT: GOSPEL-CENTERED CONVERSATION

When I'm doing a deep dive into a particular book, I have between 6-10 resources that I dig into that range from study Bibles and concordances to theological dictionaries and systematic theology books. *(See the back for my reference guide of my favorite Bible study tools.)* In this series, the goal is to supply enough historical context and theological explanation for deep understanding without crossing over into so much head knowledge that it distracts from the main message of the gospel. Should you come across something "missing" in the commentary, that likely means we felt elaborating on it would divert the conversation into secondary issues that too often divide rather than unify.

There's also a reason we chose to call this *conversational* commentary: because I want you to feel like you're sitting in my living room with a cup of coffee and an open Bible. The verse-by-verse commentary is anchored in truth about God, but His truth also invites us to lovingly respond. I loved the opportunity to include in the commentary how God has moved in my heart to obey the truth in the text.

WHAT TO EXPECT: COMMENTARY BY WOMEN FOR WOMEN

While my being a woman does not change the truth written in God's Word, it does affect my perspective, what obedience practically looks like, and the roles and experiences God has given me in my life. While these conversations and questions could absolutely be used in mixed-gender settings, I wanted to provide commentary and questions that specifically address God's design for women as well as women's roles as partners in the gospel, wives and moms -- among many others. God's Word has shaped how I see every role in my life and every place He has called me. I pray this series equips women to fulfill the Great Commission *(Matthew 28:19-20)* and to see their valuable place in God's work in the world.

WHAT TO EXPECT: MULTIPLICATION THROUGH DISCIPLESHIP

In the last letter he wrote before he was killed, Paul gave Timothy some descriptors of the Lord's servant, one being *"able to teach" (2 Timothy 2:24)*. Paul is not advocating to Timothy that all of God's servants must be skilled communicators, but that they must *know the* truth so they can *teach* the truth to others. Some have long regarded teaching merely as a spiritual gift. And while God has certainly given some the gift of teaching, teaching is more than a gift. Teaching cannot be separated from discipleship. You wouldn't have this book in your hand if you didn't feel called to know God more through His Word. But what you are compelled to *know*, you should also be compelled to *share*.

WHAT TO EXPECT: GROUP DISCUSSION QUESTIONS

Along with commentary for verse-by-verse study, I've included questions for group discussion. I've done my best to follow a formula my husband *(one of the most passionate people about discipleship that I know)* calls *peeling the onion* -- a method where the questions require more thought and transparency the deeper into the discussion you go. Specifically, each discussion begins with an icebreaker that is based on personal experience. Next, there are 2-4 questions with answers that are relatively simple to find right there in the text. Finally, the discussion concludes with another 2-3 questions that require more personal reflection, accountability and application.

If you have a spiritually mature group, you may not need to use the provided questions at all. These open-ended questions could work to guide a great discussion for each meeting:

1. *What stood out to you most? Did you notice anything for the first time?*
2. *What did this text prompt you to pray for/about?*
3. *Based on what you read, what action do you need to take in your life to obey what you learned?*

A note of encouragement: The discussion will get easier as your group meets with more frequency. It's normal for conversation to be quieter in the beginning, so don't be discouraged if it feels like you're doing a lot of the talking when your group is new. Make it your goal to talk less each week and make sure you're waiting long enough after you ask a question before you jump in to answer it yourself. Moments of silence feel longer when you're the one initiating the conversation – so be okay with a few pauses in conversation. Someone will jump in eventually, and the silence gaps will get shorter as your group becomes more comfortable with one another.

As noted at the beginning, though, discipleship is not merely words. Bringing people in closer to you will provide you with opportunities to demonstrate the gospel through your care for them and your actions in general. These moments are not secondary to your time spent teaching. Take the time to love deeply. As my pastor, Bruce Frank, says all the time, "Declare *and* demonstrate the gospel."

Praying for you and your group! May God speak powerfully to us through His Word.

In Him,
Michelle

CONVERSATIONAL COMMENTARY ON 2 TIMOTHY:

Before You Read 2 Timothy

What's on your mind before you die? I know, a bit heavy and morbid for an intro, but the truth is, there's a reason why we are fascinated by someone's last words. People don't talk about meaningless things when they know their time is short – and that's the lens with which we get to read 2 Timothy. Knowing his death was inevitable, Paul wrote his final letter – his last written words – to Timothy, a pastor who was like his spiritual son.

Paul was no stranger to prison, but this time was different. Late in the letter, Paul describes his conditions. But you would never know that behind these bold words, full of faith, confident hope and unwavering endurance, is a man who was cold, lonely and awaiting execution.

These four chapters are saturated in truth, encouragement, practical theology, and personal instruction: the foundation of the gospel, the importance of sound doctrine, a warning about false teachers, the necessity of gospel community, examples of what to do and what *not* to do, requirements for being a faithful disciple in a broken world – Paul covers everything that matters and ignores everything that does not.

But beyond **what** was on his mind, 2 Timothy gives us insight into **who** was on Paul's mind:

Jesus

The gospel was carrying Paul through the harsh conditions and loneliness of the Roman prison. Throughout the letter, Paul preaches to himself as he teaches Timothy. He consistently comes back to the hope we have and the promise of eternal life because of Jesus.

The reminder for us: **Keep Jesus on your mind.** Remembering Jesus is the only way to truly gain proper perspective for every circumstance.

Timothy

By the time he wrote 2 Timothy, Paul's ministry resumé would have been quite impressive. But reliving his accomplishments or the vastness of his influence are nowhere to be found in this letter. Paul realizes his legacy will be best passed on, not by trying to reach the most people, but simply by telling Timothy, so Timothy will tell others.

The reminder for us: **God's assignments often come in people form.** The most important things you do in your life will not be big tasks or grandiose achievements, but the investments you make in the people God puts around you. Go deep with people. Trust God for width.

If we do that, then maybe we'll reach the end of our lives and be able to look back like Paul did and say:

> **"I have fought the good fight, I have finished the course, I have kept the faith."**
>
> 2 TIMOTHY 4:7

Paul Snapshot:

- Born as a Roman citizen and trained as a Pharisee
- Also known as Saul of Tarsus
- Persecuted Christians and participated in the martyrdom of Stephen *(Acts 7)*
- Converted to Christianity on the road to Damascus *(Acts 9)*
- Preached Christ faithfully for three missionary journeys
- Wrote letters to churches and believers that later became 13 books of the New Testament
- Worked as a tentmaker to financially support his ministry
- Remembered as the greatest missionary of all time and the apostle to the Gentiles

Timothy Snapshot:

- Raised in faith by his mother (Eunice) and grandmother (Lois)

- Like a spiritual son to Paul

- Often traveled with Paul or was sent by Paul to serve as his representative at other churches

- Became pastor of the church at Ephesus

2 Timothy Fast Facts:

- Written around A.D. 64-67 likely 2-4 years after 1 Timothy

- Paul is writing to Timothy from prison in Rome. Several of Paul's imprisonments were relatively comfortable, but that's not the case for this one. In the letter, he writes of being cold and lonely, missing the companionship of fellow believers and time together in God's Word.

- The last written words of the apostle Paul before his execution

Gospel Connection:

Another work in the Conversational Commentary series is **Ecclesiastes: Wisdom to Live for Heaven While on Earth.** Ecclesiastes was written by Solomon, near the end of his life. Paul and Solomon lived their lives in opposite order: Solomon started strong but didn't finish well. Paul didn't have a strong start, but he had a faithful finish. While their lives looked drastically different, they both came to the same conclusion at the end of their earthly lives: **God and everything He does is what matters. Nothing else does.** But when you come to that conclusion with joy like Paul versus regret like Solomon, you communicate that truth differently. If you haven't already studied Ecclesiastes with us, it's powerful to examine these two men looking back on their lives and legacies back-to-back. If that interests you, dig into Ecclesiastes next!

Challenge:

You may be used to studying longer passages of Scripture for each group meeting, but it really is incredible how much encouragement, truth, theology, and practical application is packed into these four chapters of 2 Timothy. Read the text slowly and really examine each word or phrase. *(In most cases, the commentary will guide you to do this!)* It's not wrong to study the same verses over and over again – even several days in a row. These words contain truths we will never master outside of the power of God. I am praying during your study of 2 Timothy for you to experience Hebrews 4:12 in a personal way: *"For the word of God is **living** and **active** and **sharper** than any two-edged sword, and **piercing** as far as the division of soul and spirit, of both joints and marrow, and able to judge the thoughts and **intentions of the heart**."*

🐝 *Lord, speak to our hearts as we come to Your Word. Help us fight the good fight for a faithful finish. Amen.*

2 Timothy 1:1-18

COMMENTARY

1:1   Near execution, Paul is first, writing a letter to Timothy, but he's also preaching to himself. By identifying himself as an apostle of Christ Jesus, he reminds himself of his purpose here on earth. Especially since he's near execution, the phrase *"by the will of God,"* reminds him that his circumstances are not driven by those who threw him in prison or those who will execute him, but that all of his days were ordained by God. By referencing the *"promise of life in Christ Jesus,"* Paul is clinging to the truth that his best days are yet to come in heaven. He has hope, confident that his earthly death does not mean his life is over, but that his eternal life, made possible through the death and resurrection of Jesus, is about to begin.

1:2a   Because of Paul's missionary journeys, he started dozens of churches. His influence, without question, was vast among believers both then and now. But for his final written words, Paul wasn't thinking about the crowd or about reaching the masses himself. Timothy, a pastor who Paul had mentored since he was young, whom he lovingly refers to as *"his beloved son,"* was the one on his mind. God's assignments often come in people form, not just in tasks. A life that is marked by the gospel invests in others and doesn't just love casually or conditionally; it loves others like family.

1:2b   Before Paul gave Timothy any of his words or wisdom, Paul reminded Timothy what he already has and will always have from God the Father and Christ the Son: grace, mercy and peace. Basically, Paul is saying, *"Let's remember Who makes everything else I will say in this letter possible. Nothing I'll say has any weight without what God made possible through Jesus."*

1:3   Because of their commitments to the gospel, Paul and Timothy are not serving in the same city. Paul is in prison, and Timothy, who hasn't been arrested, is continuing the mission of sharing

Christ, mainly in Ephesus, where he is the pastor. I'm sure if they could have, they would have stayed serving together, but God gave them assignments that did not allow them to continue to serve together. Obviously, in prison, Paul is limited in how he can share the gospel, compared to other times when he moved about freely, preaching and planting churches from city to city. But even though he's limited in how he can serve, Paul is reminding himself that he's still serving God, even in chains. Because he has people planning to kill him, he's being accused and labeled as "guilty." So his *clear conscience* doesn't come from his earthly approval rating but from his confidence that he is following God. He refuses being resentful over his current circumstance by remembering Timothy, who is still moving the mission forward, in his prayers. In your earthly relationships, when distance keeps you apart, prayer can keep you connected. And when your circumstances are hard, praying for others helps you see the bigger picture of God at work so you won't just dwell on your situation and feel sorry for yourself.

1:4   Acts 20:17-38 records Paul's farewell to his leaders at Ephesus, Timothy included among them. Luke *(the author of Acts)* is a detail guy, so we don't have to imagine what Paul means by recalling Timothy's tears. Acts 20:37-38 gives us a picture of these grown men weeping and embracing, desiring to soak up every last second together so much that the men actually *got on the ship* with Paul before he left. I imagine that when they actually started drifting away from the dock, they stayed on the ship as long as they could before they had to jump off and swim back to shore. Once again, this illustrates that ministry is about souls, not accomplishments. My dad is a pastor, and when I was growing up, he would frequently say something along the lines of, *"Ministry would be so easy without the people... but people are the point."* Others – not achievements, numbers, titles, or any other form of notoriety – bring joy to your ministry. Like Paul writes, let your gratitude for God drive you to pursue people.

1:5a   Before he acknowledges any gift that Timothy has, Paul recognizes that what will help Timothy endure to the end, as he has, is sincere faith. Scripture defines faith as, *"the assurance of things hoped for, the conviction of things not seen"* (Hebrews 11:1). Faith is confidence in the future we have because of Christ – not a skill set that we can see or merely belief in something that has already happened. Knowing the ups and downs Timothy will experience in life, Paul is emphasizing faith as the one thing that will always get him through. Don't put your confidence – for yourself or others – in what can be seen. What will create curiosity and continue to impact lives, including your own, for eternity is sincere faith.

1:5b Your home life can have a serious impact for the gospel. Paul, though he has mentored Timothy and certainly seen him grow tremendously in the Lord, knows that the first seeds of faith that were planted in Timothy, were from his grandmother, Lois, and his mother, Eunice. I doubt when Timothy was super young that these women ever thought that their son would be a pastor, let alone be personally mentored by the man who would go down as the greatest missionary of all time. But still – they were faithful to their God-given assignments of mom and grandma – and look at what God did through their obedience. Like Lois and Eunice, God will not waste the unseen *(and likely unpraised and unthanked)* ways you serve your family.

1:6 In the phrase *"For this reason,"* Paul acknowledges God's goodness to plant the seeds of the faith in Timothy's heart at a young age. Rather than pointing out new gifts Timothy needs to acquire or strengthen, Paul reminds him that the same God he trusted as a little boy already put in him what he'll need to endure until the end. *"Kindle afresh"* is this picture of continuing to come back to God to get the next "spark" he'll need. Paul aims to convey the importance of both Timothy's confidence in God and continual dependence on God, not himself or merely the gifts God has given him. Don't focus on "finding" your gift; God already gave you one. Pursue courage and perseverance to continue using what He gave you.

1:7 Upon belief in God, we get access to the Holy Spirit – not a spirit of timidity or fear. Power, love and self-discipline are all the work of the Holy Spirit. The Holy Spirit's power is why our weakness is usable to God – because *His power is made perfect in weakness* (2 Corinthian 12:9). We don't merely have to muster up love on our own – *we love because He first loved us* (1 John 4:19). And self-discipline/self-control is so much different than willpower – it is making efforts so the "self" that exists in all of us yields to the Holy Spirit – *so we walk by the Spirit instead of gratifying* *our flesh* (Galatians 5:16). Again, Paul isn't reminding Timothy of something else on his to-do list, but reminding him who God has made him to be by the power of the Holy Spirit.

1:8-10   These three verses are a beautiful summary of the gospel. But let's not forget the original author and audience – a seasoned pastor is sharing the gospel with a seasoned pastor. Why? First of all, the gospel that saves us is the same gospel that will *sustain us*. We don't just need to hear the gospel one time. We need to hear the gospel over and over again to continue taking steps of faith and obedience here on earth. Remind yourself and remind others of the gospel – no matter how many times we hear it, we never outgrow needing to hear the gospel.

1:8   Whenever you see "therefore" in Scripture, it should prompt you to ask the question, "What is *therefore* there for?" *Therefore* is always a reminder that whatever was said before connects to what is being said next. So after Paul reminds Timothy of who he is through the Holy Spirit's power in verse 7, even if he is persecuted because of Jesus, Paul then reminds him he is equipped to stand up for the truth of the gospel without fear. The path has already been paved. The work has already been done. Because God is real and Jesus finished the work on the cross, we can confidently walk in what God has already given us and what Jesus has already done. Even if it produces a form of suffering on this side of heaven, there's no pain on earth that can compare with the glory coming ahead in Heaven with God. Basically, Paul is telling Timothy, "*Keep preaching Jesus, and when it's your turn to suffer, the Holy Spirit will supply you with what you need to endure.*"

1:9   Word order really matters in verses like this. It's one of the reasons why I love the NASB *(New American Standard Bible)* translation for deep study. The NASB is a transliteral translation, which means it mirrors the original language as closely as possible. [Full transparency: it's not as readable and doesn't always flow as well as some other translations.] But that's because Greek sentence structure is very different from English in that it doesn't flow in a consistent order like ours of "noun, verb, direct object." In Greek, the most important words were listed first. So, in understanding the foundation of the gospel, we see that:

1) God saves us. More than us making a smart decision, God is the hero, and without Him, salvation is not possible.

2) Once we're saved, we're *called*. Calling is not merely a word for pastors and preachers, but all those whom God saves are called to join Him in His work in the world. The highest calling that we will ever have this side of heaven is to be His disciple and live on mission.

3) God's gift of salvation is precisely that – a gift – which means it cannot be earned. God saves us, through Jesus alone – because of His purpose and grace – not our works. And that is the gospel.

1:10   A pastor, Jonathan Pokluda, once shared this powerful statement on his Instagram account *(@jpokluda if you're on IG and want to follow!):* "The apostle Paul entered heaven to the cheers of those he martyred. That's how the gospel works." Reading Paul's letters, particularly this one, it's hard to picture that the man writing is the same Paul who once persecuted Christians. But because of Jesus, Paul's past, as well as every sin ever committed – including yours and mine – are exchanged for Jesus' righteousness when we believe in Him. That's the incredible power and the amazing grace of the gospel!

1:11   Paul didn't choose to be a preacher, an apostle, and a teacher in his own power or skill sets. God appointed him. The same is true for you. Wherever you are, God has plans to use you there – *because of the gospel.*

1:12   Even though Paul is in prison, awaiting execution, he is confident God is in full control. He does not let his circumstances, even his upcoming undeserved death, affect his faith and belief in Christ. In fact, by saying *"God is able to guard what I have entrusted to Him until that day,"* Paul recognizes that the people who kill him aren't capable of taking his life because he already gave his life over to God.

1:13   Even in the same generation when Jesus walked on the earth, the gospel was already being distorted. Some took away from the gospel. Others added to it. The charge that Paul gives Timothy, that we need to take to heart ourselves, is to stay grounded in the truth of the gospel because of our faith and love for Christ.

1:14   The *"treasure"* Paul tells Timothy to guard is the gospel. Really think about that word "guard." Paul is telling him to protect it. Defend it. Hide it deep in his heart – just as we should too. Frequently, Paul uses the words *"remember"* or *"remind"* in his letters. More than something new or something we don't yet possess, most of the time, what we really need is to be reminded of what God has already done or what God has already said. Paul even points out that the best way for us to guard our hearts with the gospel is through the Holy Spirit – not simply our own ability to remember. The Holy Spirit's ministry highlights the work of Jesus. Pray for the Holy Spirit to help you remember what Jesus has done.

1:15-18   Paul finishes his urgent plea for Timothy to cling tightly to the gospel with real examples of what *not* to do – Phygelus and Hermogenes – who once believed but turned away from the gospel. But he also shares an example of what to do - Onesiphorus – whose love for Paul was unaffected by his current circumstance. I love the word Paul uses to describe his visits: *"he often refreshed me."* We often refer to ministry relating to the gifts God has given us, but there's huge ministry to be done that's simply wrapped up in your presence. You don't have to say the right thing, do the right thing, or fix the thing. Sometimes, ministry is literally just being there *for* someone and *with* someone who is going through something hard. Don't neglect to show up because you don't know what to say or do. Just be there. Also, note that Paul is aware that from prison, there's nothing he can do to repay Onesiphorus back for his kindness – but he's also confident God can. That's the kind of faith I desire: a faith that knows even though my time on earth is limited, I can still say prayers now that God is capable of answering after my time on earth is over.

2 Timothy 1:1-18

QUESTIONS

Icebreaker: Who is someone you consider to be family, even though you are not actually related? Tell us one thing that makes your relationship with this person so special.

1. Paul was an influential person for many – then and now. Yet, when it came to his last words, he realized the best way to reach the most people wasn't to write a letter to the masses, but to write a letter to Timothy, so Timothy could tell others. This letter serves as a gentle reminder for us that God's assignments often come in people form. Who are some of the people in your life right now that you see as part of God's assignments for you?

2. 2 Timothy 1:5 is a sweet reminder of how your home life can have a serious impact for the gospel. The majority of the ways you serve your family will be unseen – and likely unpraised or even unthanked. Our flesh, that longs to be recognized, could easily get resentful. But since intimacy grows in small spaces, these unseen moments are more like moments between us and the Lord that He will be faithful to use and one day reward – far from insignificant tasks that don't make a difference. What's one practical way you can have more of an eternal perspective in your daily rhythm of passing on sincere faith to your family?

3. Read 2 Timothy 1:8-10 aloud. Re-visit the commentary for these verses and discuss the basic truths of the gospel. Even though the gospel is simple to understand, what do you think holds people back from accepting God's free gift of salvation through Jesus?

4. Do you ever feel like in order to share your faith, or even to encourage fellow believers, that you need to have something new to say? Does it take some pressure off of you to realize that rather than hearing something new, more often than not, we just need to be reminded of what God has already said and Jesus has already done? Personally, when do you most often need to be reminded of the gospel? Share with your group so you can remind each other!

5. Because of the gospel, Paul was appointed a preacher, an apostle, and a teacher. What would verse 11 look like if you personalized it for where God has appointed you? What is the difference between living appointed by God vs. simply existing in the places God has you?

6. Practically, what are some ways you guard the gospel in your life? What are the possible dangers and distractions if we don't make efforts to guard the gospel in our hearts? What are some ways others distort the gospel by taking away from it or adding to it?

7. 2 Timothy 1 ends with Paul's gratitude for Onesiphorus – someone who simply eagerly searched for him and came to visit him while he was in prison. He couldn't get rid of Paul's chains, but he could sit with Paul while his chains were on. We live in a fast-paced world where it seems the ministry of presence – just showing up and being there for each other – happens less and less. How do you think it would demonstrate the gospel to those around us if we simply showed up for one another more? Who is someone you can show up for this week?

2 Timothy 2:1-7

COMMENTARY

2:1   *"You therefore, my son"* – Remember the question we should ask when we see *therefore* in Scripture – what is *therefore* there for? After Timothy remembers the gospel, remembers who God really is and what Jesus really did, Paul can give him some more instruction and encouragement. This should serve as a great reminder for all of us as we invest in others – the gospel should always be our foundation. Every other piece of advice or teaching we offer should flow from the foundation of the gospel.

"be strong in the grace" – Do not try to live in your own power. Think about it: human logic regards strength and grace in opposition. Strength and grace don't normally go together – unless you're not drawing from your own power, but relying on His. Human strength/power will almost always steamroll. It will not be graceful. The only way for your strength to be graceful is for you to be fully dependent on God.

"that is in Christ Jesus" – Relying on God's power means we put our full trust that He will supply the grace and strength we need to do His work. But we need to remember that through Christ, we get access to His grace and strength – but it's not to accomplish our own agenda. Being strong in the grace that is in Christ Jesus is for the sole purpose of joining God in the work He is already doing.

2:2   The sign of being an effective teacher of the gospel is not merely marked by drawing bigger crowds to listen to you teach. It's when those who listened to you teach are compelled to go share the gospel with others. It's not about gathering more students, but actually making disciples. Culture measures by addition – *how many followers do you have? How many people are in the audience?* God's Kingdom measures by multiplication – *how many were sent out to join you in teaching others about God?* In the same way, we were never meant to be merely listeners of the gospel. We shouldn't consume the gospel, but the gospel *should* consume us. What we hear from our faith mentors, we should share with others. Really consider that word *"entrust"* Paul uses to describe what happens as the gospel leaves our mouths and enters into the hearts of others. *"Entrust"* communicates both relationship and responsibility. Aim to have other believers pouring into you, while you pour into others – not just one or the other. God could have chosen so many ways to communicate the gospel to the lost world, but He chose to use us. We need Jesus most, but we need one another also.

2:3-6   In these four verses, Paul uses three different analogies to illustrate some practical ways we follow Christ: as a soldier, an athlete and a farmer. All matter to us as we follow Christ, but you will likely go through seasons where one of these will be especially challenging. In a soldier season, you must have a wholehearted commitment and be willing to sacrifice. In an athlete season, you must train for godliness with the guidelines that God gives us in His Word. In a farmer season, you must work as hard as you can, patiently trusting God for the results.

2:3   Think about the process of becoming a soldier: soldiers enlist, then head to bootcamp, where they are isolated from all distractions and maintain a disciplined regimen to prepare them for battle. Soldiers know that when the battle begins, they may be called to lay down their lives for the sake of the mission. Soldiers cannot be half-in, fearful or selfish. In the same way, following Christ will require courage, commitment and sacrifice. That's why Paul's first words here are, *"Suffer hardship with me."* Following Christ will not always be easy, but we can trust that it is worth it.

2:4   It would be very easy to misunderstand this verse and read it in such a way that makes us think we are to distance ourselves from the world. But truthfully, we are the ones that tend to make clear distinctions between the spiritual and secular. God never does. As a follower of Christ, *everything* you do is meant to be spiritual – because of Who you follow. From working a corporate job, playing on a community softball team or simply grocery shopping for your family – all of those things can be spiritual – not because the task or the place is spiritual, but because *you are*. What Paul means is as you go about your normal life, living in this world, don't allow yourself to get caught up (*"entangled"*) in what the world values. Consider how easy it is to get caught up in the world's affairs - we have access to it from our thumbs! We can get caught up in arguments and in the brokenness around us. We can certainly get caught up in the evil that exists ourselves, or we can simply get distracted because the world provides so many different options of what to do, what to believe, and how to live. But it's not just about what we get caught up in that's so bad in itself. When we're caught up in what the world offers, we miss our opportunity to join God in His work in the world. We miss our chance to obey and please the One who *"enlisted"* us. We're not meant to merely live our lives in a way that tries to avoid evil. We are to actively participate in God's mission.

2:5 *"Winning"* in the Christian life centers around obedience – not merely being first to finish or strongest in skill. The athletes Paul refers to here are Olympic-style athletes. Highly disciplined, these athletes train day after day, repeating the same skills and drills over and over again. But when it comes time for the race or the event, whether they win or lose doesn't merely come down to how perfectly they trained. In order to get the crown, they have to follow the rules: stay within the boundaries, not starting too early, crossing the right finish line, etc. Even a slight step out of bounds could cost an athlete the race. The athlete who gets the crown knew the rules and obeyed the rules. But here's where this gets tricky. Yes, God has given us commands to obey, and obeying God is critical to following Him. But the rules don't drive our obedience – our love for the Lord does. Because we love God, we respond to Him in obedience. If we bend toward simply following rules, we could miss the relationship we're designed to have with God. But if we focus on the relationship and ignore the rules, that's not being loyal in the relationship – which doesn't actually make it a relationship at all. Aim to avoid the extremes – and obey God out of an overflow of your love for Jesus.

2:6 The keyword here is *"ought."* Farmers work long hours doing difficult tasks. Farming is physically demanding and requires an incredible amount of delayed gratification to see fruit from your labor. Even in the off season from cultivating crops, there is a ton of preparation to get the land ready. So, because of all the hard work, farmers "ought" to be the first to benefit from their work. But here, Paul reminds Timothy that things don't often happen as they "ought" to or as we think they should. Life will not always work out in ways that seem logically fair. We must be willing to take the back seat. This is especially challenging for us because culture constantly dishes out "you deserve this" language. We have to be so careful because our flesh, that has a natural bend toward entitlement, won't often stop at *"this is what should happen"* but it will evolve to *"this is what I deserve."* We must issue ourselves a *hard. stop.* in those moments. Think ahead to the moment when you will stand before a holy God -- you do not want what you deserve (And praise Jesus, nor will you get what you deserve if you are in Christ - because of God's grace!) Because of Jesus, we get heaven – which we do not deserve. So when it comes to following Jesus, be prepared, be patient, and be content to work as hard as you can, resting in whatever outcome God chooses.

2:7   God will always help you to understand… but you won't be able to get there on your own. James 1:5 reminds us that if we lack wisdom, we can ask God and He will graciously supply it. When it comes to the things of God, which is the way we are called to live, you cannot expect yourself to understand it on your own – and this is actually *really* good news. Isaiah 55:8-9 reminds us that God's ways and God's thoughts are infinitely above our own – which is why He is worthy of our worship. A God that thinks exactly like you or me wouldn't be worthy of worship. Because He acts in ways beyond our understanding, we can trust that He is truly God. And remember – you can trust God even when you do not understand. Keep trusting, ask God for understanding, and He will give it to you.

2 Timothy 2:1-7

QUESTIONS

Icebreaker: What's something you've been taught that you haven't been able to keep to yourself? *(a certain skill, a piece of advice, etc.)* Or what's something you have personally taught someone else that you would love for them to pass on or share with someone else?

1. Before Paul offered Timothy any advice, he laid the foundation of the gospel first – which should remind us that any instruction or advice we provide should flow from the foundation of the gospel. What are some key ways to identify if our advice and teaching is grounded in the gospel?

2. God could have chosen so many ways to communicate the gospel to the lost world, but He chose to use us. What we learn about God, we should share with others – and it doesn't have to look like a formal teaching setting. It's just allowing others to invest in us while we invest in others. Thinking about the truth in 2 Timothy 2:2 – what do you need prayer and accountability for most? To take the time to listen? For courage to share?

3. It would be very easy to misunderstand 2 Timothy 2:4 and read it in such a way that makes us think we are to distance ourselves from the world. But truthfully, we are the ones that tend to make clear distinctions between the spiritual and secular. God never does. As a follower of Christ, *everything* you do is meant to be spiritual – because of Who you follow. Everything you do can be spiritual – not because the task or the place is spiritual, but because you are. How does this change your mindset for the places God has you?

4. Paul also uses the analogy of being an athlete as we follow Christ in 2 Timothy 3:5 to illustrate that in the Christian life, winning centers around our obedience. But more than simply obeying out of obligation, we obey out of an overflow of our love for Jesus. What are some ways we can identify if our obedience is driven by love and our relationship with God or if our obedience/disobedience is simply about the rules?

5. In his final analogy, in 2 Timothy 3:6, Paul compares following Christ to being a farmer and what "ought" to happen after the farmer's hard work. Do you ever feel the tension between the *"you deserve this"* language from culture when things in your life don't work out how they "should?" In those moments, how do you let go of your entitlement and trust God instead?

6. Have you ever stopped to consider that it's really good news that we can't understand God without His help? Because His ways and His thoughts are so much higher than ours, He is worthy of our worship. What are some things you're struggling to understand right now? Share with the group, and pray for God's wisdom for each other.

7. Of the three analogies above – which one is most difficult for you to put into practice right now? Are you having a hard time being a soldier in this season and need wholehearted commitment and a willingness to sacrifice? Or are struggling to be an athlete – training for godliness as you follow the guidelines God has set for you? Or are you battling a farmer season right now – one where you are working really hard and doing your best to patiently trust God with an outcome that you wouldn't have picked? Be honest about how you're struggling, and pray for one another.

2 Timothy 2:8-21

COMMENTARY

2:8 Those first three words – *"Remember Jesus Christ"* – are the solution to the majority of the problems we encounter here on earth. In everything you do, in everything you say and in everything you are, remember Jesus Christ. If you're having conflict with someone else, remember Jesus Christ. If you think you deserve something you're not getting, remember Jesus Christ. Have this phrase on repeat so much that it becomes like a song you can't get out of your head.

Remember who Jesus is. By describing Jesus with the phrase *"risen from the dead,"* Paul is reminding Timothy that Jesus was fully God. By using the phrase *"descendant of David,"* Paul also describes Jesus as fully man. Those two phrases – fully God and fully man– are key in understanding the gospel. In being fully God, Jesus was able to satisfy the wrath of God for sin and conquer death through His resurrection. And in being fully man, He was able to be our substitute, living as our perfect example without succumbing to sin Himself. The Jews were expecting the Messiah to come from the lineage of David *(as prophesied in Jeremiah 23:5-6)*, and His resurrection was proof that Jesus is the Son of God.

Remember what Jesus did for you. First, note how personal the gospel is to Paul. He doesn't write *the* gospel but instead, writes *my* gospel. Jesus' death on the cross that satisfied God's wrath for sin once and for all was for all of us, but it was also *just for you.* God knows you intricately. He knit you together in your mother's womb *(Psalm 139:13)*. He loves you so much that He paid a great price – His Son's life – so you would have the opportunity to put your trust in Him, have Jesus' righteousness added to your account and live eternally with Him in Heaven. When you remember Jesus, don't let yourself solely think about Him in a way that considers what He did for *everyone*. Remember what He did for *you.*

2:9-10   Paul is in prison, awaiting execution, because of his commitment to the gospel. But despite his circumstance, Paul knows that the mission of the gospel can continue – because even though he's in chains, God's Word is not. Paul may be being treated like a criminal, but Paul's ministry isn't over. Scripture contains many records of when Paul was imprisoned and shared the gospel with other prisoners and his guards *(Acts 16, Acts 24-28, to name a few)*. We may not have the specific details of this imprisonment, but because of Paul's perseverance, we can guess this time in prison is no different. Just because you're not sure how it would even be possible for ministry to happen where you are, you can make a gospel difference anywhere you go – just as Paul did in prison. You may be restricted, but God is not. It is *"for this reason"* that Paul endures the false accusations, the persecution, and the harsh conditions of the prison. Despite it all, he is confident in the gospel. He knows his future in heaven, made possible by what Jesus did, is secure. Paul knows that his refusal to give in to the high official's demands or his own temporary well-being will strengthen the faith of others. Like Paul, we should be far more concerned with the eternal comfort of others than our own earthly comfort. Also, be confident that what you do for Christ continues without you. Elisabeth Elliot once put it this way: *"You can never lose what you have offered to Christ."* For Paul, it was the churches he planted and the people he invested in, like Timothy whom he is writing to. The same is true for us. Offer every area of your life to God, and even when you are gone, God can continue to use what you did during your life for His glory. In verse 10, Paul also highlights two important truths: 1) Salvation is found through Jesus alone. 2) Through Jesus alone, we can have eternal life.

2:11   When we are in Christ, death does not get the final say. Jesus does. If you've ever been reading in the New Testament and gotten confused when someone dies and Scripture says they "fell asleep," that used to confuse me too. But "falling asleep" is actually a much more accurate way of looking at death as believers. Death is not permanent; like sleep, it's temporary. Confessing Christ in our earthly life secures our eternal life with Him in Heaven. Because of Jesus, death is not the conclusion of your life. Death may end your earthly life, but earthly death also begins your eternal life.

2:12a   Endurance – not performance – is what is rewarded by God. Anything that we think would merit a reward *(probably something we can measure - like being better than someone else or how many tasks got completed)* is not a factor for how

God rewards. Remember the words we all long to hear one day from God? "Well done, my good and **faithful** servant..." *(Matthew 25:21;23)*. With our fleshly bent toward comparison and competition, it would be easy for us to tack on additional requirements – even with semi-good intentions. But finishing *first* or finishing *best* is not what God rewards. He rewards endurance. We should prioritize what God rewards.

2:12b   These words echo words Jesus said Himself, recorded in Matthew 10:32-33: *"So everyone who acknowledges Me before men, I also will acknowledge before My Father who is in Heaven, but whoever denies Me before men, I also will deny before My Father who is in Heaven."* It further emphasizes that our eternity is not determined by how many good things we do, how much we know about God or the Bible, etc. – but merely our answer to the question: **What do you believe about Jesus?** Your answer to that question is the most important decision you will ever make. Believing in Him – that He is the Son of God, that His finishing work on the cross was the necessary payment for your sin, and that His resurrection is proof that Jesus alone can offer you eternal life – is crucial to be claimed as His.

2:13   This verse is like a hug with a warning. Paul reiterates the faithfulness of God. God does not go back on His Word. We can always trust that God is who He says He is and that He'll do what He says He'll do. In a world that constantly changes, it's insanely comforting to rest in the truth that God is the same yesterday, today and forever. But part of embracing that truth requires that we recognize that the decision we all make about Jesus will determine where each of us will spend eternity. Even though God went through great lengths to provide a way for us to get back to Him after sin caused the separation between us, those who choose not to believe in Jesus will be separated from God forever. God's desire is for all to be saved *(1 Timothy 2:4, 2 Peter 3:9)*. Isaiah 30:18 reminds us that He longs to be gracious to us. But despite His desire to be gracious and for all to be saved, God cannot deny His faithfulness. Those who die with Him will live with Him. Those who endure will reign with Him. And He will deny those who deny Him. If you are reading this and you're not sure what you believe about Jesus, stop and pray right now. Ask God to reveal Himself to you. He longs to be gracious to you - He will!

2:14   *"Them"* in these verses refer to the people Timothy was shepherding because he is the pastor at the church in Ephesus. *"These things"* refer back to everything Paul has shared with

Timothy up to this point in the letter – which mainly has pointed back over and over again to the gospel. Because division is often easier than unity, Paul reminds Timothy to let the gospel serve as an anchor for him. Basically, Paul reminds him, "Don't ever get too far away from the gospel." Paul is also beginning a conversation, contrasting what Timothy knows to be true of the gospel with the twisted version of the gospel being shared by false teachers. He then extends the charge further to the people under his care, but not on Timothy's authority or Paul's authority, but on God's authority – to encourage them to use the gospel as a guardrail in their conversations too. In terms of charging them not to *"wrangle about words,"* the main application for Timothy is to stop arguments over theological controversies, which were largely being stirred up by false teachers. You can read more about our commitment to this in the *Introduction to Conversational Commentary* section at the beginning of this book, but our aim is to write commentary that highlights the gospel and minimizes conversations *(or more likely - arguments!)* on secondary issues. This verse is a huge reason why we have such strong convictions on this – because secondary issues – *defined as any issue that does not directly impact where someone spends eternity* – are often called secondary issues, but they're rarely treated as such. So whether you're having a conversation with a believer or an unbeliever, if you're trying to discern if a conversation about Jesus or spiritual things is an important conversation or merely a theological controversy, you could ask: **Would it make sense to weave in the gospel to our conversation?** Because if the gospel wouldn't fit, it's probably not a beneficial conversation to have. Our spiritual conversations should never get so far away from the foundation of our faith that it would be difficult to transition to the gospel. Always be willing to defend the gospel, but don't waste your time with other theological arguments. Even if a resolution of agreement were to be reached, arguing over theological issues doesn't gain any real Kingdom ground – so it *"ruins"* its hearers because it wastes the limited time we have on earth being wrapped up in a conversation that doesn't really matter. I love teaching the Bible – that's why you're reading these words. But my prayer is that my life is defined far more with seeing souls saved by God and lives transformed by the gospel - not merely me teaching the Bible to make saved people smarter or to give me something to do while living comfortably in a Christian bubble.

2:15   Diligence implies consistent earnestness and attention. But note where Paul charges that our diligence should go – *"to present yourself approved to God."* The motivation for our diligence matters. We shouldn't be diligent to impress others, to lead others, or to somehow prove ourselves worthy. But instead, your diligence should recognize you are not here to please people. God's opinion and approval is all that matters. Make efforts to dwell on God's opinion of you far more than anyone else's and join Him in the work He's doing. Continuing his warning concerning false teachers, Paul also encourages Timothy to stay committed to the truth of God's Word. This seems to be difficult at times, since our human minds are not capable of fully understanding everything God does. That's why false teachers can draw large crowds: they make a habit of twisting what God has said so the human brain can understand it without faith. My pastor, Bruce Frank, always puts it this way: "When you and God disagree, God's right, you're wrong, and by His grace, you can change." Ask God to help you trust even if you don't understand. One of my favorite verses that I think shows what following God practically looks like is in Mark 9:24. Jesus asks a father whose son has an unclean spirit if he believes that He can heal his son, and the father says, *"I believe. Help my unbelief!"* Use that prayer in the moments when you feel stuck between doubt and faith. Read your Bible, and then, let your Bible read you. Study your Bible so you know the difference between what's worth defending and what's a distraction.

2:16   In addition to staying away from theological controversies, stay away from worldly conversations that have no benefit and will lead to *"further ungodliness."* A conversation is never just a conversation. Words are never just words. Luke 6:45 puts it this way: *"Out of the overflow of the heart, the mouth speaks."* Our words reveal the posture of our heart and the center of our affections. And our words can quickly stir up more ungodliness: anger, pride, envy, hatred, bitterness, etc. Obviously, as Christians, we've never been great at this, since Paul is already addressing this issue with people who had actually lived in the same days as Jesus. But in a digital world, the "in-fighting" between Christians has escalated to a new level. The content of our arguments has likely not changed much, but the distribution and public consumption of it has. And public discussions, like the disagreements between believers on social media, are not merely theological discussions. These discussions *(that become ugly quickly and produce that further ungodliness Paul warns us about here)* become our witness to a lost world. How will the lost world be able to see Jesus in us if such a huge part of what they see is our ungodliness being produced by our worldly chatter?

2:17   Paul doesn't hold back on the strength of his analogy. He
compares these kinds of arguments to cancer. Cancer spreads
quickly and affects your health beyond the area where it's
concentrated. Cancer cells steal health from the body. And the
gospel is the only cure and remedy for healing. The gospel
promotes love and unity and highlights what God has already
done for us, while these arguments only provoke anger
and division.

2:18   We don't know much more about the controversy other than
what is shared here, but basically, these men were elevating
what's happening here on earth over what we will experience
in eternity. This wasn't the only controversy happening among
believers at the time, but this one example shows us how easy
it is to take the truth of the gospel and twist it. That's why it's so
important that we be grounded in God's Word for ourselves - so
God can speak straight to us and we can identify both His truth
and the enemy's lies when we hear them.

2:19   In one verse, Paul highlights both the sovereignty of God and
our human responsibility to walk in what we know to be true. No
matter how many arguments take place or how much evil seems
to temporarily prevail, God's truth will stand. God is in full control.
Our actions do not dictate God's response. God has already
responded to us by sending Jesus. But our response to what God
has done for us is what is required from us. If we believe in Him,
we should respond with obedience, not wickedness. But here's
the important thing: we don't obey *so* God will love us. We obey
God *because* He loves us.

2:20-21   Think about your house. No matter how large it is, you have
various containers that hold different things. Maybe you have
fancy china you registered for when you got married displayed
in your dining room for its beauty. Maybe you have a decorative
bowl that is displayed on your coffee table, a fire-proof safe that
contains important documents, or maybe an antique trunk of
family heirlooms. But in addition to the "containers" that you
proudly display or protect, your home also has a trash can, a
toilet, or maybe a junk drawer or closet that you pray no one
will ever open. In this powerful illustration, Paul is showing how
we are God's vessels. If we choose to display the gospel and to
make the gospel the contents of our lives, that's the equivalent
of being a gold or silver vessel that's *"honored, sanctified, useful
to the Master, prepared for every good work."* But if we choose
to display the non-gospel issues, holding on to arguments and
unprofitable discussions, we make ourselves the equivalent of

"earthenware" and *"dishonor"* – aka *a trash can!* As a believer, you have the opportunity to display the most beautiful story this world has ever seen – the gospel. Let's be intentional to live our lives in such a way that displays the gospel – not garbage.

2 Timothy 2:8-21

QUESTIONS

Icebreaker: Do you have a drawer, a room, – maybe it's even your car – that is so cluttered that you pray no one sees it? *(If you watched Friends, Monica's closet is your example!)* We promise we won't look – but tell us the messiest place in your life currently.

1. Read the first three words of 2 Timothy 2:8 and stop. Those three words are probably the solution to the majority of the problems we encounter here on earth. As a group, collaborate on a list of times and circumstances when it would do you *(and those around you!)* the most benefit if you would *"remember Jesus Christ."*

2. In your own words, explain what Paul means in 2 Timothy 2:9 that though he is imprisoned, *"the word of God is not imprisoned."* Maybe you feel like you have restrictions in a secular job of how much of the gospel you can share or you have a strained relationship that doesn't currently give you much opportunity to share truth with someone you love. How does this truth give you hope and remind you of the difference between what we can do and what God can do?

3. 2 Timothy 2:12 reminds us that God rewards endurance. His reward is not attached to your performance. Related to the truth in this verse, how would you describe the difference between endurance and performance? What are some warning signs that would let you know that you may be striving more for performance than endurance?

4. Read 2 Timothy 2:11-13. Also, have different group members read 1 Timothy 2:4, 2 Peter 3:9, and Isaiah 30:18. Despite His desire to be gracious and for all to be saved, God cannot deny His faithfulness. Those who die with Him will live with Him. Those who endure will reign with Him. And He will deny those who deny Him. Truly, the most important decision we will all make is what we believe about Jesus – because it determines where we spend eternity. How do these verses comfort you? How do they challenge you?

5. 2 Timothy 2:14 encourages us not to *"wrangle about words"* because it's useless and leads to ruin for its hearers, and 2 Timothy 2:16 challenges us to stay away from *"worldly and empty chatter."* Knowing Paul was never one to run from conflict when it came to defending the gospel, what do you think are the differences between a truth that's worth defending and an argument that's not worth having? How do we know the difference? Do you think the content of the conversation is all that matters, or does the place where these conversations take place matter too? As you read these verses, what ways come to your mind for how we can apply the truth from Paul's words here today?

6. Read 2 Timothy 2:15. What should our motivation be for our diligence? Why does our motive matter? In the midst of encouraging Timothy to stay grounded in God's Word, Paul also mentions the names of several false teachers who had twisted the gospel. What are some ways the gospel gets twisted today? What are some ways we can protect ourselves against false teaching?

7. Using a powerful analogy between gold and silver vessels that would have been used for celebration and distinguished guests vs. vessels of wood and earthenware that would have served mainly as toilets and trash cans, Paul makes a distinction between believers who display the gospel and others who hold on to arguments and unprofitable discussions. How do these secondary issues – issues that do not impact where someone spends eternity – distract us from our main mission? Why do you think we have such a hard time distinguishing between gospel issues and secondary issues? Do you have a secondary issue that you know you need to personally yield to the gospel?

2 Timothy 2:22-26

COMMENTARY

2:22a   In the same thought, Paul articulates what we should run away from *and* what we should run toward. This illustrates the truth that living a life for God is not merely a matter of sin avoidance but actively pursuing what is good.

What we should avoid: youthful thoughts and desires, which can practically be summarized as anything that falls under the categories of selfishness and pride. Even though running away is sometimes categorized as avoidance, let me assure you: it does not make you *weak* to run from immature thoughts and ideas; it's *wise*. So many times, Scripture uses the analogy of how living for Christ is a battle. In a battle, it's just as important to know when to run as it is to know when to fight. Don't entertain the immature thoughts your flesh conjures up, run from them. God has called you to be part of His work in the world, so you don't have time for immature things.

What we should pursue: righteousness, faith, love and peace.

Righteousness: God's righteousness is wrapped up in His character and actions. Because we are called to be imitators of Him *(Ephesians 5:1)*, God sets the standard for what we should aim to be - not merely trying to be more righteous than one another. Yield to and race after His righteousness.

Faith: Hebrews 11:1 defines faith as *"the assurance of things hoped for, a conviction of things not seen."* Faith is not full understanding *of* God, but full trust *in* God. Faith is your confidence that Christ died for you, defeated death, and one day, will return for you so you can live with Him forever in Heaven. Biblical literacy is important, but we must remember that God didn't tell us, "Learn everything you can about Me," or "Understand Me." But He says, *"Believe in Me" (John 14:1)*. Pursue activating your faith.

Love: 1 Corinthians 13 defines love by our actions, not merely feelings. God's definition of love requires patience, kindness, refusal of its own way *(just to name a few!)* – traits we will not pursue if left to our own power. But 1 John 4:8 reminds us that love is more than something God does; God *is* love. Pursuing love starts with pursuing God Himself. Not solely His benefits, but understanding that pursuing God will transform everything you do. Matthew 6:33 assures us – if you seek Him first, He will take care of everything else.

Peace: Peace is wrapped up in God's presence – not an absence of conflict. God is our peace *(Ephesians 2:14)*. In the moments when you find yourself the most distressed and unsettled, pursue time with the Lord. He is all you need for peace – and unlike the world gives, He gives His peace to us freely and forever *(John 14:27)*.

2:22b Because the first part of this verse is so full of truth and application, it would be easy to gloss over that word "with" that connects these two ideas together. Yes, we are supposed to flee from immature thoughts. Yes, we are supposed to pursue righteousness, faith, love and peace. But we're not supposed to flee and pursue alone – but alongside other believers. Your salvation is personal. No one else can make that decision for you. But we're not called to live out our faith in isolation. In fact, going all the way back to the beginning when God was creating the world, everything He made – the land and water, night and day, sun, moon and stars, plants, animals and man – God said it was good. But the first time God recognized there was a problem in the perfect world He created and said something was *"not good"* – is when He recognized Adam was alone, and He was moved to create Eve *(Genesis 1:27)*. God designed us for community. The markers of being His disciples are love *(John 13:35)* and unity *(John 17:23)*. Love and unity – neither one can be displayed alone - they require another person. Our commitment to living in community with one another is so important that when culture rises up to let us know that we should "just be yourself," our confidence as believers should remind us: **You can't be yourself by yourself – not your fullest self that God created you to be.** Be in a gospel community connected to a local church - it's a critical part of your witness and your discipleship.

2:23 I don't have to tell you how noisy the world is. We literally always have a way to share our thoughts and opinions. And listen – to those of you who have a lot of opinions – I get you; so do I. So good news – I'm not telling you to not have opinions. But I will encourage you to recognize this: most of the time, your opinion doesn't matter. Your opinion isn't needed. And just because you *have* an opinion, that doesn't require you to *share* your opinion. You don't need to get involved in every conversation. Because here's the truth: the more opinions you share, the more arguments you will have – and arguments do not stir up godliness. Stay focused on the gospel and what God has called you to do instead. Train yourself so when a personal opinion pops up in your brain, you can immediately think, *"And my opinion doesn't matter."* That one way of renewing your mind will have a tremendous impact on helping you to stay focused where God has called you.

2:24a   We can't skip over the title Paul uses for us as Christ-followers: *"the Lord's bond-servant."* That's our role. That's our title. Really think about that for a moment. How would it affect your relationships and interactions with others if you were to replace whatever earthly role or title you have with *"the Lord's servant"* instead? How would it change your marriage if you thought of yourself as the Lord's servant in that relationship? Your parenting? Your career? Your neighbors? Your friends? If you have some extra time, get a sheet of paper and list your roles and relationships. Then, spend some time in prayer, asking God to help you to primarily view yourself as His servant in that place or for that person. Bottom line: as a believer, your primary role in the lives of others is to be God's servant. The next word of this verse is just as important: *"must."* The instructions that follow in the next two verses are not optional if we are aiming to be the Lord's servant. It's not up for debate. In order to be the Lord's servant, these are the traits and actions that are required of us.

2:24b-25a These two verses give us five non-negotiable traits of what the Lord's servant does. Before we dive into each of these traits individually, let's look at them collectively. Together these traits are a combination of love and truth. Often, love and truth are described as opposites, but in Christ, they cannot be separated. Ephesians 4:15 reminds us to speak the truth *in* love – it's not one or the other. Love is how we handle the truth. Paul David Tripp once explained it this way: *"Truth isn't mean and love isn't dishonest."* You probably have a natural bend toward one or the other – either love is easier for you or truth is easier for you. Whichever one is less natural, pray about it. Without love, truth is just noise *(1 Corinthians 13:1-2)*. And without truth, love is just an emotion. Here's a deeper look at the five traits of the Lord's servant:

1) must not be quarrelsome: In case we didn't get the point earlier of how important it is that we stay away from arguments, Paul lists this trait first. Aim to be a peacemaker. Don't be easily angered. Overlook minor offenses. Don't say things or do things that stir up division and arguments. Romans 12:18 says, *"If possible, so far as it depends on you, be at peace with all men."* Others may attempt to stir stuff up with you, but you do not have to participate. Be a peacemaker.

2) be kind to all: Throughout your life, you will always have people who are easy to be kind to and people who are *not* so easy to be kind to. That's why the distinction *"to all"* is so important – because the level of ease shouldn't determine our level of our kindness. Whether it's easy or hard, whether we *always* agree with this person or we *never* agree with this person, whether kindness is reciprocated or not, whether kindness comes naturally or whether you have to beg God every second to be kind through you – we should show the same level of kindness to everyone. When it comes to being the Lord's servant, kindness is always required.

3) able to teach: This does not mean that all of God's servants must be strong and skilled communicators. Remember Moses - He had a stutter *(Exodus 4:10)*. Zero microphones or audience required. This simply means that if we are going to be the Lord's servant, we have to know what He says. And we don't attempt to learn what He says solely for our own knowledge, but we learn His truth so we can obey His truth and so we can teach His truth to others.

4) patient when wronged: The ESV translation translates this phrase as *"patiently enduring evil."* When someone wrongs you, be patient through it. In this world, we should expect to be wronged. It shouldn't catch us off guard. Broken people act broken. Saved people are still sinners who desperately need a Savior. Choose patient endurance over anger or entitlement. Extend the same grace to others that has been extended to you. Refuse to retaliate. Instead, respond to evil with love. Even if the grace you give doesn't appear to be noticed, your decision to be patient when wronged will be a gentle reminder for a fellow believer and generate curiosity in the person who does not yet know God.

5: with gentleness, correcting those in opposition: First, note that of the five traits to be the Lord's servant, being willing to correct others is mentioned last. We often want to jump to correction, but Paul reminds us that our correction must display all of the other traits mentioned first. All truth that you administer must not be quarrelsome, it must be kind, it must be patient, and it must be gentle. Gentleness is mentioned before correction. Your gentleness is the most important part of any correction you give. You've probably experienced this yourself: it's hard to receive corrections that aren't presented with gentleness. It's far more important that your correction is *heard*; not merely that your correction is *said.*

2:25b　This should bring you a big sigh of relief. Your job is not to convince anyone of the truth or to bring anyone to repentance. Conviction is God's job. God opens our eyes to truth. God grants repentance. Understanding the gospel is what helps us to be transformed into a new creation *(2 Corinthians 5:17)*. But here's where the tension comes in: Just because God is the One who convinces others and changes lives, that doesn't mean you and I merely sit around and wait on Him to be sovereign. God's job is salvation and repentance, and our job is to not be quarrelsome, be kind to all, be able to teach, to be patient when wronged, and with gentleness, to correct those in opposition. Be His servant. That's your job. You *must.* Here's two things I can promise you: Following Him means God is the Lord of your life. What He says goes. His way over your way. Every. Single. Time. Think about this through the analogy of parenting. Every parent sets rules for their kids. And sometimes, the kids don't like the rules the parents set. But as loving parents, we don't set rules for our kids because we love *rules.* We set rules for our kids because we love our *kids!* As our perfect Father, God is the same way with us. He gives us ways to obey Him because He knows what is best for us. You will be miserable in your walk with the Lord if you don't live in obedience to what He asks you to do. Another fact: you'll also be miserable if you attempt to do His job and neglect to do yours. Speaking from experience, let Him convince. Let Him bring others to repentance. He is always faithful to do His job. Trust He will do it.

2:26　I love the phrase *"they may come to their senses."* Because God created each one of us, anyone who is trapped in the devil's snare has literally lost their senses. One or the other will be true of us: we will either be under the power of the Holy Spirit, or we will be under the influence of the enemy. This is why following Christ isn't a half-hearted commitment. That's why as Paul writes these words, he's giving instructions to the Lord's *servant* and insisting that we *must.* Because in being the Lord's servant, we won't simply *know* the truth; we'll *handle* the truth His way and we'll gladly do the job He's given us.

2 Timothy 2:22-26

QUESTIONS

Icebreaker: What is a rule that your parents had for you growing up or a decision they made on your behalf that you didn't agree with at the time, but now, you realize it was actually the best thing for you?

1. Read 2 Timothy 2:22. What does Paul say to avoid? What does Paul say to pursue? Do you ever think of living for Christ more in terms of sin avoidance instead of recognizing what we're supposed to pursue? As you read the commentary and studied on your own, what stood out to you most?

2. 2 Timothy 2:22 also points out the importance of not trying to live for Christ on our own. Discuss this sentence from the commentary: "When culture rises up to let us know that we should just "be yourself," our confidence as believers should remind us: **You can't be yourself by yourself – not your fullest self that God created you to be.**" How does this influence how you view the importance of gospel community?

3. Read 2 Timothy 2:23. Have you experienced it to be true that the more opinions you share, the more arguments you have? Why is it so important that we recognize that even if we have opinions that our opinions really don't matter? What's one practical way you stay focused on what God has called you to do instead of getting distracted by your opinions?

4. Read the first three words of 2 Timothy 2:24. How would it affect your relationships and interactions with others if you were to replace whatever earthly role or title you have with *"the Lord's servant"* instead? Have everyone in the group share one role or relationship where you will intentionally practice being the Lord's servant this week. *(Pray for and check in with whoever is seated to your right at some point this week!)*

5. Read 2 Timothy 2:24-25 aloud. As a group, list the five traits Paul says the Lord's servant must have. From your study this week of these five traits, which one stood out to you most? Which trait

comes the most naturally for you, and which one do you need to work on most?

6. 2 Timothy 2:25b highlights how ultimately, God is the one who brings others to repentance - not you or me. Practically, what does it look like to be willing to correct someone with gentleness but trust God will be the one to convince them and bring them to repentance? How can you remind yourself of the difference between God's job and your job?

7. These verses truly do highlight how truth and love do not compete with one another - in Christ, truth and love always work together. We all have a natural bend toward one or the other. Which one comes more naturally to you – love or truth? How can you use your natural bend as a strength? How do you need to be careful to also prioritize the area where you are naturally weaker?

2 Timothy 3:1-9

COMMENTARY

3:1   The *"last days"* began when the Spirit fell at Pentecost. Acts 2:17 says, *"And in the last days it shall be, God declares, that I will pour out my Spirit on all flesh, and your sons and your daughters shall prophesy, and your young men shall see visions, and your old men shall dream dreams."* But this truth actually dates back further than Acts – this verse references Old Testament prophecy found in Joel 2:28-29. As exciting as it sounds to think that God's Spirit is poured out on us so we can prophesy, see visions, and dream dreams, Paul reminds us that the last days will also highlight the broken world around us. When sin entered the world, it forever changed God's relationship with mankind. That's why God sent Jesus to earth – to make a way for us to be restored to Him, since we could never get back to Him on our own. Here's the reality, though: it would be easy to be discouraged by all the brokenness around you. As Paul writes here, it's difficult. Sin creates all sorts of problems that affect us. But this world is not our *home*, so it's not our *hope* either. We should be burdened by the broken world around us, but by the power of Christ, it doesn't have to break us. Like Paul displays here, we must live with an urgency for the gospel, recognizing our time on earth is short.

3:2-9   In these verses, Paul paints a picture of our broken world. If you'd walk around Target for 10 minutes, you'd gather all the evidence you need that every word he wrote is true. In verse 4, Paul tells us that we are to avoid being like this. Just a few verses ago, Paul reminds us, though, that following Christ is not merely about what we avoid, but what we pursue. *(See commentary note on 2 Timothy 2:22)* So as we look at these descriptions of how people will behave in the last days, the commentary below will discuss it from both lenses: what we should *not* do and what we *should* do. As JD Greear put it once: "If you want to make a difference, you have to be different."

3:2-4   **Instead of being *"lovers of self,"* love God and others most.**
Matthew 22:37-40 is coined "The Great Commandment" because

in these verses, Jesus says the greatest commandment is to love God and to love others. We are born selfish. Parents don't have to teach their children to say, "Mine!" if someone grabs their toy. Selfishness is the natural human reaction. So if we want to look different from the world, we can't be consumed with ourselves and our own desires. Genuine love for God will prompt us to love Him and want what He wants – and that same love for the Lord will overflow through us to others. Loving others is not a different love you have to muster up on your own. Rather than just looking out for yourself and your own interests *(Philippians 2:4)*, look for opportunities to love others *through* the love of Christ.

Instead of being *"lovers of money,"* love generosity. This doesn't mean we should avoid money altogether, but avoid *loving* money. We should get far more joy from giving to others than getting something for ourselves. Four thoughts on this: 1) Don't wait to be generous until it's "wise." Scripture doesn't make a distinction between being generous if you have a lot of money or a little money. It simply calls us to be generous – period. 2) Wealth isn't evil in itself. But because money is a top competitor for our hearts, Jesus never talked about wealth without a warning, so we shouldn't either. Recognize that wealth could easily cause you to rely on your money instead of God. 3) Remember that everything belongs to God anyway – including your money. Take the example of tithing: When you view money as God's and not yours, instead of struggling to give Him 10%, you'll feel blessed He lets you keep 90% of what is His. 4) Live in such a way that how you view and use your money grows your faith more than your bank account. Faith growth is the only growth that lasts – so let faith be your bottom line, not your money.

Instead of being *"boastful"* and *"arrogant,"* pursue humility. Arrogance desires the appearance of being better than you actually are; humility has confidence Jesus is better. My pastor, Bruce Frank, pointed this out and I've never forgotten it: nowhere in Scripture does God tell us to pray for humility, but simply to be humble. Humility is a pursuit. In its simplest form, humility is the daily pursuit of making Jesus more. In John 3:30, John the Baptist says, *"He [Jesus] must increase, but I must decrease."* Elevate Him with your praise and refuse to elevate your self-importance.

Instead of being a *"reviler"*-- one who speaks with contempt – encourage others. However, we don't want to cheapen encouragement to affirmation - there is a huge difference!

Encouragement is not flattery. When you encourage someone, you literally put *courage* in them. Each of us needs courage to obey God in our lives. We need courage to step out in faith and do what He's called us to do. Use your words to strengthen the faith of others. Show up for others in ways that will increase their confidence in God. In 1 Thessalonians 5:11, Paul affirmed a church who was doing this well - encouraging each other and building one another up. The world often tears down; build others up instead.

Instead of being *"disobedient to parents,"* obey your parents. You're never too young to live on mission for Christ. Children who choose to follow Christ don't have to wait to be an adult to be His representative. Kids and teens are a pivotal part of how we display Christ and the difference He makes in our lives to a watching world! They can make a huge difference in schools and among their peers – simply by going against rebellion culture and choosing to obey their parents. If you're reading this and your parents don't believe in Jesus yet, I know it sounds crazy, but one of the best ways you can show Christ's love to your parents is through your obedience. Try it! Also, obeying the earthly authorities God has given you – like your parents – helps you to cultivate a heart of obedience to Him too.

Instead of being *"ungrateful,"* be grateful. Instead of being consumed with what you don't have, choose gratitude over entitlement. Knowing what others have is easier now than it has ever been. Without a renewed mindset, it's easy to bend toward being dissatisfied with what we don't have instead of being grateful for everything God has given us. I love this encouragement Paul tucked into his letter to the Philippians. He writes, *"I know what it is to be in need, and I know what it is to have plenty. **I have learned** the secret of being content in any and every situation, whether well fed or hungry, whether living in plenty or in want. I can do all this through Him who gives me strength" (Philippians 4:12-13).* Contentment didn't come naturally to him; contentment was something Paul had to learn. We must learn contentment too. The best first step? Ask God to teach you contentment while you practice gratitude.

Instead of being *"unholy,"* be holy. Holiness and perfection are not the same. Pursuing holiness means that we take seriously the identity we have in Christ as a new creation *(2 Corinthians 5:17).* While we wait to be made fully new in eternity someday, we get to live in our new identity now – as sons and daughters of God. In Romans, Paul talks about how we will either be slaves to sin or slaves to rightousness *(Romans 6:18)*. Holiness determines how you handle your sin. God takes our sin seriously, so we must take sin seriously too. As you pursue holiness and walk in your new identity in Christ, when you fall short, you can repent *(which literally means to change directions!)* of your sin and rush back to God. Does your sin grieve you and lead you to rush to God in repentance for His forgiveness and grace? Or do you find yourself covering your sin up, trying to justify it, and running from the Lord in shame?

Instead of being *"unloving,"* be loving. Plain and simple: if you can't do it with love, don't do it. If you ever find yourself resorting to pride, hate or shaming someone else because you believe that's the only way you can get your point across, forget your point and walk away instead. Choosing to make a point will often rob you from making a difference. Why? Because love is so much more than a feeling. Love is our proof that we belong to Jesus *(John 13:35)*. If love is how we will be known, love can't take a backseat to winning the argument. Demonstrate the gospel by choosing to love someone extravagantly, especially when they don't deserve it. Again, this doesn't mean compromising truth. But we must remember that both of these statements are true: **Compromising love compromises truth. Compromising truth compromises love.**

Instead of being *"irreconcilable,"* choose Jesus. By definition, *irreconcilable* means "representing findings or points of view that are so different from each other that they cannot be made compatible." In our relationships with other believers, we are called to unity. So even if you disagree strongly with another believer on a particular issue, if you agree on Jesus, He is enough for you to pursue unity. As for our relationships with those who do not know Christ, we are still called to love. You can disagree with someone and still love them. Bottom line: don't be labeled by anything other than Jesus. Don't cut yourself off from relationships – with both believers and unbelievers – over an opinion.

Instead of being *"malicious gossips,"* forgive as you have been forgiven *(Ephesians 4:32)*. In Christ, God no longer sees you for what you've done. So because you have been forgiven, when you look at others, don't see them for what they've done. Sin does harm on its own, and gossip only adds to the collateral damage. Really think about it: what good can gossip possibly do? Gossip not only puffs up your own pride, but it heaps more shame on a person... and God doesn't shame us. The Holy Spirit convicts us, but conviction is loving correction for the purpose of bringing someone back to God, while the enemy uses shame to provoke running *from* God. When you are made aware of something that someone has done, care for them if you are able, pray for them, and stop any malicious gossip that comes your way.

Instead of being *"without self-control,"* control your "self." That is not a typo. There is a difference between controlling yourself and controlling your *self* – as in your flesh and your selfish nature. We have to be careful to not cheapen self-control to willpower. Somer Phoebus, my ministry partner and best friend, once put it this way: "Self-control is a funeral for your flesh." Following Jesus is accepting a call to self-denial. Daily, you deny yourself, pick up your cross, and follow Him *(Luke 9:23)*. Galatians 5:16-24 is one of my favorite passages that calls us to walk by the Spirit as a means to not gratify the flesh. But there's really only two ways that this will flush out: we will either deny our flesh or we will gratify it. Spend a few moments in prayer concerning this: *are you denying your "self" or seeking to satisfy it?*

Instead of being *"brutal,"* be compassionate. My favorite example of this is in John 8:1-11 when we get to see Jesus' interaction with a woman caught in adultery. *(Go re-read it quickly if you have time!)* The Pharisees brought this woman to the temple courts to be stoned, because that was the custom based on Old Testament law. Jesus wrote something on the ground, and when He spoke, He said, *"He who is without sin among you, let him be the first to throw a stone at her."* And they began to go out one by one, *"beginning with the older ones" (John 8:9).* I point out that the older ones left first because I see this in my own life – the longer we walk with Christ, the quicker we are to dismiss self-righteousness when it rears its ugly head. When Jesus addressed the woman, he said, *"I do not condemn you either. Go. From now on, sin no more" (John 8:11).* Compassion does not mean ignoring sin or condoning sin. Jesus was the only one with authority to condemn her, but He chose compassion. We should too. To the ones who have been walking with Christ longer, be quick to show compassion to set an example for those who are younger. (And be patient with the young ones too!) When you find it difficult to be compassionate, ask the hard question: *Am I demonstrating self-righteousness or Christ's righteousness?*

Instead of being *"haters of good,"* love what is good. Sadly, unbelievers tend to know more about what Christians are against than what we are for. Maybe this is because instead of loving what is good, we try to hate what is evil. But our attempts to hate evil typically only come across as hate. Consider Jesus on the cross. Jesus stood up to the evil surrounding Him with the greatest display of love this world will ever see. Like Jesus did, let's love what is good and trust that His love stands up to hate so much more powerfully than merely hating evil.

Instead of being *"treacherous,"* be honest. In the original language, the word Paul uses here refers more to deceit than danger. Think about it: why do we lie? Most of the time, it's either to gain something we didn't earn or to protect ourselves against some form of pain. No matter how many times we see this play out, we seem to forget that lying only complicates the circumstance more, and the truth usually comes out anyway. [A couple of examples: Abraham and Sarah before Abimelech *(Genesis 20:1-16)* and Rebecca and Jacob before Isaac *(Genesis 27)*.] Be aware if you find yourself using phrases like *"exaggerating the truth"* or changing what really happened *"for someone's own good."* No one likes to admit to lying or being deceitful, so your pride will probably look for ways to make your dishonesty sound wise. Be honest with yourself, and be honest with others.

Instead of being *"reckless,"* act with eternity in mind. Typically, when we act recklessly, we are reacting to something that is temporary. But because of our identity in Christ, we get to respond to the world from God's perspective instead of our own. We are to *"set our minds on the things above, not on the things that are on the earth" (Colossians 3:2)*. Think with Heaven in mind, not the temporary. Aim to take God's view of your life and what's in it – not merely what you can see.

Instead of being *"conceited,"* worship God. Worship Him. In addition to reminding yourself of who God is, worship puts you in your place too. When you are in awe of God, there's no way to be in awe of yourself. You will have the most accurate view of yourself when you stay as close to Jesus as you can.

Prioritize God over pleasure. Pleasure will always cooperate with your pride. Pleasure often shows up in *"I need this"* or *"I deserve this"* language. Pleasure doesn't like to wait; pleasure wants it now. Loving pleasure more than you love God often will cause you to seek getting your needs met outside of the boundaries God sets for you. Aiming to love God more than you love pleasure doesn't sign you up for a life of misery – but demonstrates that you are willing for your desires to yield to His desires. Loving God more than pleasure means you desire what He wants for you more than you merely just want what you want.

3:5   This belief is still common today. Some actually label themselves as believing in universalism theology – the belief that all religious paths result in salvation and everyone can simply pick their path. Others simply say something like, "Jesus works for me, but you can pick what works for you." Both are examples of *"holding to a form of godliness"* but denying God's power in that Jesus' death on the cross was the payment for sin and that His resurrection served as proof that He is the only way to Heaven. The free gift of salvation is available to all *(John 3:16-17)*, and salvation is possible only through Jesus. There is no other way. Jesus said it Himself: *"I am the way, and the truth, and the life. No one comes to the Father except through Me"* (John 14:6). Any version of the gospel that does not recognize that Jesus is the only way to heaven denies God's power. Also, be wary of anyone who appears spiritual or religious, but there is no evidence of God's Word in their mouth or His work in their lives. [See commentary note on 2 Timothy 3:10-12 for more on this.]

3:6-7   Here, Paul's indirect warnings about false teachers gets much more specific. False teachers prey on certain kinds of people: those who are covered in shame because of their sin; those who follow their feelings and their flesh *("various impulses")*; and those who are in a perpetual state of learning but never arrive on firm beliefs and convictions. This has not changed today. But beyond looking to see who they're talking to, the key indicator to identify a false teacher or a false gospel is the answer to this question: **What do they believe about Jesus?** False teachers and false gospels will always minimize Jesus. Every other religion is rooted in what you have to do, but the gospel is rooted in what Jesus did for you. There's no way to minimize the role of Jesus in the gospel. Jesus changes everything.

3:8-9   In Exodus 7, Aaron displays God's power by casting down his staff and having God turn it into a snake. Pharaoh responds to this by having his sorcerers *(Jannes and Jambres)* do the same. Although Aaron's snake literally eats the other two snakes, Pharoah still was not moved to believe in God and would not let the Israelites go. A similar situation occurs in Exodus 8:16-19, but this time, the outcome is different. Jannes and Jambres attempt to recreate the power of God with their own magic, but they cannot. They even confess to Pharoah, *"This is the finger of God"* (Exodus 8:19). Even if false teachers appear to "succeed" for a little while, it will not last. And ultimately, as a minister of the gospel, remember that they are not opposing you; they are opposing God. That is a whole different category of opposition. Stay focused on sharing the gospel, and let God deal with them. He will.

2 Timothy 3:1-9

QUESTIONS

***

Icebreaker: Any product that has been out for a while generally has the original version with many knock-offs that follow. Either tell us about a knock-off you've discovered that's so good, we'd never know it wasn't the original –or– share your favorite original product that's so good, we should never fool with the knock-off version.

1. Read 2 Timothy 3:1-5 together. As you read Paul's description of the broken world, what thoughts come to your mind? Practically, what do you think it looks like to be burdened for the broken world we live in while making sure our hope stays grounded in Christ?

2. Was it helpful for you to think about Paul's description of the broken world in a way that reminds us how we can live differently to make a difference? What stood out to you most from the commentary notes on 2 Timothy 3:2-4?

3. Because Paul includes *"disobedient to parents"* in his description of the broken world, that reminds us that kids and teens who have chosen to follow Christ have an important role in the mission of God. What are some ways you can encourage your kids to live on mission for Jesus now instead of feeling like they have to wait to be an adult? *(For the parents, this would make a great conversation to have with your kids this week!)*

4. Read Philippians 4:11-13 as a group. Do you agree that contentment is something we must learn? Who teaches us contentment? What are some things God has shown you that have helped you learn to be content?

5. In your own words, describe the difference between controlling yourself and controlling your *"self."* The difference between gratifying the flesh and denying your flesh? *(Refer to Galatians 5:16-24 if you have extra time!)*

6. Has it been your experience that more unbelievers you meet know more about what Christians are against than they know what we are

for? Do you agree that hating what is evil typically comes across simply as hate? Personally, what is one way you aim to "love what is good" instead of hating what is evil?

7. Read 2 Timothy 3:5-9. What reminder was most helpful to you in how to identify false teachers or a false gospel?

2 Timothy 3:10-17

COMMENTARY

3:10 So often, when we think about what discipleship is, we reduce it to merely teaching. And while teaching is part of it, discipleship is so much more! Because this follows Paul's conversation about false teachers in previous verses, these verses make a distinction between what false teachers and false gospels do and say versus what Timothy has experienced for himself and seen modeled by Paul. When you disciple someone, they should be able to follow your–

"teaching:" Discipleship is not *merely* teaching, but teaching is part of it. But remember, don't associate "teaching" with being a skilled communicator. [See commentary note on 2 Timothy 2:24.] Teaching is about your commitment to learn God's truth and share God's truth with others. Teaching is your willingness to have conversations about Jesus with others. To the church at Corinth, Paul said it this way one time: *"Follow me as I follow Christ" (1 Corinthians 11:1).* Discipleship involves you teaching others what God has taught you – not your own content or opinions. Open God's Word together, talk about what it means, hold one another accountable, and pray for each other as you do so.

"conduct:" If teaching is *talking* about what we believe, conduct is *behaving* how we believe. Think about it: there's no shortage of gospel-centered content that people can easily access. From podcasts to articles to full church services being streamed on demand online, gospel-centered content is more easily accessible now than it has ever been. But when you look around, does the world appear more sanctified? Nope. Hear me out: I am certainly not against gospel-centered content. But sometimes, I wonder if the availability of good content has made us lazy in the role God gave each of us to play. Not that we behave badly per say, but if we rely heavily on the best-selling authors and pastors of big churches to reach the lost, that mindset neglects The Great Commission *(Matthew 28:19-20)* that Jesus commanded to all believers. The best person to reach those you have influence over with the gospel isn't necessarily the strongest communicator – it's

you! It makes a powerful difference when you get to hear the truth from someone, then live in close enough proximity to them to also watch them walk it out.

"purpose:" If someone were to look at your life, what would they say you're about? That's your purpose. As believers, Jesus is our purpose. Jesus is the connecting thread of our lives and considered in everything we do and every decision we make. When someone is in a discipleship relationship with you, they get to see the difference Jesus – your purpose – makes in every area of your life. From your marriage, your parenting, your friendships, your career, your interactions with strangers, how you spend your time, where your joy comes from, how you handle difficult circumstances, your purpose influences it all. Purpose is also what guides our discipleship relationships to get really practical in what following Jesus looks like on a daily basis.

"faith:" Where *(or more accurately, with whom)* do you place your trust? Faith is full trust – not full understanding. In fact, our faith gets activated, especially in the moments when we don't understand. Scripture defines faith as *"the assurance of things hoped for, the conviction of things not seen" (Hebrews 11:1).* Faith is confidence in what God has done in the past and what He'll do in the future. For someone to be able to follow your faith, you must let them in close enough to see the difference your faith makes in your life. A story that illustrates this is when Jesus heard John the Baptist *(His cousin)* was beheaded. *[You can read the full story in Matthew 14:1-21].* Obviously grieved, Jesus aimed to get away by Himself, but the crowds followed Him. When He arrived ashore and saw the crowds, Jesus had compassion on them, healed the sick, and performed the largest miracle of His ministry - feeding a crowd of 5,000 people – when all He had was a little boy's lunch. Why do you think the crowd gathered when they knew Jesus was grieved? I doubt that many people just wanted to check on Him. I'm guessing they were curious about what Jesus would say and do now. I think they wondered if His story would change after the news of His cousin's death. Our faith will always guide how we respond, but people will likely be the most intrigued by and influenced by your faith when they see you rely on it when it doesn't make sense.

"patience:" Would someone want to follow your patience? *(Did that step on your toes the way it does mine? Ouch!)* In our flesh, we are all impatient. We don't like to wait through commercial breaks, long lines or in traffic – and we don't like waiting on God's timing either. But the truth is, the Christian life is one of

waiting. In the Old Testament, they waited on the Messiah. And now, we wait for Jesus' return. Every day, we live in the tension of the *already* and the *not yet*. Just think about Jesus' ministry. He was never in a hurry, and most of His miracles occurred in the midst of an interruption. What if you chose to see the interruptions that occur in your life as God's intervention instead of an interruption? Instead of seeing life's delays as something happening *to* you, what if you saw them as something happening *for* you? When we read in Scripture, God often shows up in ways we wouldn't expect. Why would we expect our lives to mirror something different? Plus, you can always remember that you're never simply waiting *on* God - you get to wait *with* God. He will never leave you or forsake you.

"love:" Understood correctly, love is infinitely more than a feeling or an emotion. Because Jesus said we would be known by our love for one another *(John 13:35)*, love demonstrates our understanding of what God has done – not just our knowledge of it. How deeply we love isn't a personality trait or a spiritual gift; it's our testimony that tells others and shows others how deeply we are loved by God. How you love is a far better indicator of maturity in your walk with the Lord than how many Bible facts you know.

"perseverance:" Be steady. This world is fickle, swinging from one extreme to another in every way possible. Your circumstances will change. Your feelings will change. But God does not change. So when everything around you seems like it's falling apart, He holds you together. Perseverance chooses to act on what we know to be true, not necessarily what we see. Keep going. Keep believing. Keep trusting. God always has a plan, and His ways are perfect. Be steady in prayer. Be steady in hope. Be steady in your words and obedience. Be steady in love. Pass on your perseverance to those around you.

3:11   *"persecutions and sufferings:"* Paul digs deeper into persecution and suffering for the next two verses, so we will too, but for now, note that what he refers to here stretches far beyond first-world problems. For example, the incident Paul mentions that occured in Lystra? Paul was stoned and left for death. [You can read the whole story in Acts 14:19-23.] Paul saying *"the Lord rescued"* him didn't mean he wasn't persecuted and he didn't suffer, but simply that he didn't die. Paul viewed the fact that he was alive to continue the work that God had called him to do as God's rescue! My pastor growing up would frequently ask us to put our hands over our hearts to feel our heart beating. Then, he would say, "You feel that? That means God isn't through with you." I don't know what you've been through, what you're going through, or the hardship that is right around the corner for you–but I know this. If you're still here, God isn't through with you. He has delivered you through it all. And while none of us would likely choose suffering, we wouldn't understand suffering without experiencing it either. Suffering helps us identify with Jesus – and I'm not sure there's a shortcut that would provide the same result. But we must remember it doesn't end with suffering. Earlier in his life, Paul wrote, "*For as we share abundantly in Christ's sufferings, so through Christ we share abundantly in comfort too*" *(2 Corinthians 1:5)*. Abundant suffering brings abundant comfort. Rest in that truth.

3:10-11 Just for an abundance of clarity - all of this goes with teaching God's Word: your conduct, purpose, faith, patience, love, perseverance, persecutions and suffering.

3:12 That word *"all"* matters. Persecutions and sufferings are not just possible - they're promised. James put the same truth this way: *"Count it all joy, my brothers, **when** you meet trials of various kinds, for you know that the testing of your faith produces steadfastness. And let steadfastness have its full effect, that you may be perfect and complete, lacking in nothing" (James 1:2-4)*. Not *if* you meet trials, but *when* you meet trials. And this phrase is key too: *"who desire to live godly in Christ Jesus."* If you choose to live half-heartedly for Jesus, you may avoid persecution. But is choosing indifference really living *godly* or *in Christ* at all? Again, this doesn't mean to prove your legitimacy, you should go looking for fights. But living for the Lord will have you moving in the opposite direction from the world. Expect your beliefs and convictions will not be the popular ones. The gospel is not what the crowds want to hear, so persecution will happen when it's proclaimed.

3:13 *"Evil men"* are those who directly oppose the gospel. *"Imposters"* refers to false teachers. It was a problem then, and it's a problem that will only continue to get worse. But consider it this way: as much as you may not look forward to persecution, don't you think it beats *"being deceived"* and *"deceiving others?"* Persecution will not occur in heaven, but being deceived by the enemy has a terrible consequence for eternity - being forever separated from God. *This* is why our compassion should always trump over our anger toward those who are far from God – both those who oppose the gospel and false teachers. Their offense is ultimately against God – not you. And why do they deceive others? They're being deceived themselves! Fight for the truth, yes, but know it's possible to fight for truth without fighting against someone. God has taught me this lesson over and over in the last decade. I remember one false teacher in particular. Thinking about her would make me so angry – and angry to the point where I knew there was no way I could spin anything I was feeling as *"righteous anger."* So I began praying for her. I prayed for God to open her eyes to the truth. I prayed God would surround her with people who know Him and could speak truth into her life. I prayed for the believers with close proximity to her to refuse to give up on her. I prayed God would do whatever it would take to get her attention. As I prayed for her, not only did God grow my compassion for her, but He humbled me. I'm so grateful to God for opening my eyes to see the truth. I'm so grateful for the believers He put around me who speak truth into my life and don't give up on me. And I'm so grateful God continues to intervene in my life to get my attention. Don't waste your energy being angry toward someone who needs God just like you did. Pray for them. God can intervene for them like He did for you. No one is too far gone for God.

3:14-15   Keep the gospel the main thing. Continuing *"in the things you have learned and become convinced of"* means that you continue to build on the foundation of what you've known to be true since you first believed. The only knowledge required for salvation is recognizing you are a sinner in need of a Savior. Jesus, God's Son, came to earth, lived the perfect life that you never could and died the death you deserved. Your belief that Jesus' death on the cross counted as the payment for your sin and your confession that Christ is the Lord of your life results in you getting to spend eternity in Heaven with God as His free gift to you. Everything else we learn builds on that foundation – not taking away from it or changing it. Paul knows that Timothy has known the truth of the gospel since he was a young child because of his mother and grandmother. [See commentary note on 2 Timothy 1:5.] Some encouragement for the parents and those who have influence over children: there is tremendous value in teaching children. They may not know everything, but if they are learning the gospel and what Jesus has done for them, you are helping them build a firm foundation for their faith they can cling to for the rest of their lives. Teaching kids is not the minor leagues or second tier – it's foundational work that transparently, is so much more difficult to receive as an adult. God is capable of anything, but many times, when people are adults, even if they have never thought of themselves as someone who has faith, their faith foundation is already built on something else. Those who accept Christ later in life don't just have to build a new foundation; they also have to tear down their existing beliefs. Don't be discouraged when you find yourself repeating the same thing over and over when teaching children. Your repetition is forming and firming up their foundation. Just as Paul writes, pointing them to God's Word will give them wisdom that leads to salvation through faith in Jesus. True wisdom points you back to what has been done for you. It made a difference for Timothy, and it will make a difference in the children that you invest in too.

3:16   All Scripture is *"inspired by God"* and *"profitable"* – both the verses that are so beautiful that you display them on your wall and the verses that are so difficult that you've never really had a conversation about them with anyone. In seminary, one of my first assignments for a class was to read the entire Bible – not for deep study – but purely for reading – during that one semester. Needless to say, I found myself reaching for my Bible anytime I had a spare moment, even if it was just to read a few verses. Not only did that one assignment establish a much healthier habit for me in how to spend spare moments, but the quick pace gave me a beautiful realization too. For our final exam, we were given a single sheet of paper. All we had to do was sign a statement, on the honor system, that we had read the entire Bible and include our top takeaway. I sat there for a moment, unsure of where to start or how I could possibly summarize my thoughts on the entire Bible with *one* sheet of paper. But then, it came to me. On the top of my paper, I wrote, "I am more convinced than ever that the entire Bible is true." I had always believed the Bible was true, but in reading it in its entirety over such a short period of time, it was clearer to me than ever before how God guided every word. We may attribute different books to different authors, but every word of it is authoritative and ultimately, comes to us from God. Therefore, we can use it: *"for teaching"* – what is right; *"for reproof"* – what is not right; *"for correction"* – to get right; and *"for training in righteousness"* – to stay right. Scripture is so much more than a book – it is God speaking to us. To hear Him, open your Bible.

Take a look and review the chart on the next page:

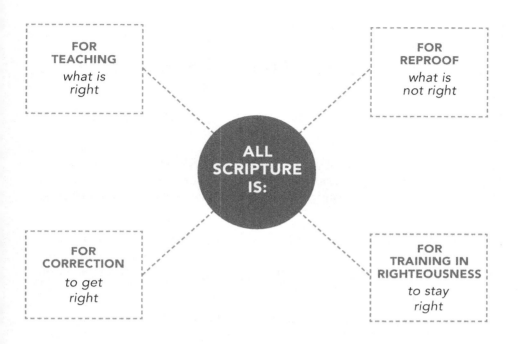

3:17 When you think of being *"equipped for every good work,"* do you think of being adequate? Or would you think that being equipped for every good work would require something more than adequacy? Let this sink in – everything you need to be equipped for every good work is in God's Word. Being fully equipped is not reserved for some, and it's not a secret either. Everything you need is right there in Scripture - fully available to all of us, so we can each be ready for whatever He calls us to do. Because that's why we read His Word – not for knowledge accumulation, but to be equipped for every good work. Reading His Word should lead to doing what God deems good.

2 Timothy 3:10-17

QUESTIONS

Icebreaker: Who was one of your favorite teachers? *(Elementary school through college – you choose!)* Why were they your favorite? Did you enjoy them simply for their teaching style, or did you admire them as a person as well?

1. Read 2 Timothy 3:10-11. Of the words Paul uses to remind Timothy of all the ways he followed him, which one do you feel like you are most comfortable with? Which one do you feel you need to work on most before someone could follow you in it?

2. Have you ever stopped to think about the fact that our world has access to more gospel-centered content than any other generation – yet it doesn't seem to be making much of a difference? Do you think we ever get lazy in the Great Commission because we believe the Christian authors and pastors will reach our lost friends? Why are you positioned to be the best person to reach someone who is far from Christ but is close to you?

3. Jesus was never in a hurry, and most of His miracles occurred in the midst of an interruption. What effect would it have on your patience if you chose to see the interruptions that occur in your life as God's intervention instead of an interruption? Can you think of some examples from Scripture when God was working powerfully behind the scenes while someone was waiting?

4. Read 2 Timothy 3:12. Who does it say will be persecuted? What should this remind us in the moments when we face persecution? What should this tell us if we never experience persecution?

5. What should that phrase *"being deceived"* in 2 Timothy 3:13 remind us about those who directly oppose the gospel and those who are false teachers? How should this help us respond to them with compassion instead of anger?

6. Read 2 Timothy 3:16. Discuss how we can use Scripture 1) *"for teaching"* – what is right; 2) *"for reproof"* – what is not right; 3) *"for*

CONVERSATIONAL COMMENTARY ON 2 TIMOTHY

correction" – to get right; and 4) *"for training in righteousness"* – to stay right. *(Refer to the chart on pg. 57 for reference.)*

7. According to 2 Timothy 3:17, everything you need to be *"equipped for every good work"* is in God's Word. Being fully equipped is not reserved for some, and it's not a secret either. Do you feel like you live like Scripture is *"adequate"* preparation? Why or why not?

2 Timothy 4:1-8

COMMENTARY

4:1   Paul was Timothy's mentor, but as he presents him with this charge, Paul doesn't appeal to Timothy with his limited authority. He charges him *"in the presence of God and of Christ Jesus."* No matter how much influence you have over someone, you are not their ultimate authority – God is. To communicate best with those in your care, consistently point to God's position in their life – and in your life too. Paul also gives Timothy a long-term perspective – that God is our judge and that Christ will return, so His Kingdom is the one that matters – even now. Keep your eyes on Jesus and what is to come. What is earthly is temporary, but what is eternal is forever.

4:2   After Paul appeals to Timothy on God's authority, he charges him with these instructions:

"preach the word:" Be about God's agenda, not your own. Stick to what Scripture says. Though it may not be the current hot topic, God's Word is always what is needed. Those who do not know the Lord need to *know* what He has done for them. Those who already know the Lord need to be *reminded* of what He has done for them. God's Word works beyond what any human is capable of speaking, so you don't have to waste your energy trying to be relevant or creative. Hebrews 4:12 reminds us, *"For the word of God is alive and active. Sharper than any double-edged sword, it penetrates even to dividing soul and spirit, joints and marrow; it judges the thoughts and attitudes of the heart."*

"be ready in season and out of season:" Convenience does not matter. Neither does comfort. Your ministry does not even need to be conventional. Consistency is what counts. *Always* be ready to minister to someone else. You probably have places where it feels more appropriate sharing your faith – maybe within the walls of your church, among other believers, or online. But this reminds us not to compartmentalize where we share our faith. The goal should be to remain the same in your words and actions as the people around you and the places you go change.

Be ready – but remember, your readiness has a lot more to do with your *willingness* than your ability. Be willing to serve God wherever you go. Wherever He takes you, He will use you if you let Him.

"reprove, rebuke, exhort:" Reproving and rebuking are both forms of correction, but reproving means to correct gently, and rebuking means to correct strongly. Paul taking the time to include both words is a reminder that we shouldn't solely use the form of correction that's easier for our personality. There are times when it's more appropriate to correct gently – maybe with a new believer or the first time a particular sin issue pops up. But there are also times when a stronger rebuke may be necessary – maybe within a close relationship, when a sin is ongoing without repentance, or when someone's actions could cause great harm to themselves or someone else. But far better than circumstances, though, to determine which form of correction to use, you will need to be sensitive to the Spirit. Strong corrections, when what's needed is a gentle one, will come off cruel. And choosing to correct gently when a strong correction is needed lets cowardice win over courage. Correction is an important piece of discipleship, but the type of correction you use matters just as much as your willingness to correct. Before you give corrections, ask God to help you know when to reprove and when to rebuke. *"Exhorting"* is to encourage. God's Word is encouraging. So if we're aiming to sound like Him, we won't just bark orders. But remember – to encourage – that's literally to *put courage in* others. Remind others of the goodness of God, of His promises, His faithfulness, and His grace. Share how He's working in your life, and share how you see Him working in their life too. Pray His promises over them. Acknowledge when you see growth in them. In parenting, I refer to this as "catching my kids doing something right." It's easy to notice when something is wrong, isn't it? We typically expect what is right, so we don't always pay attention to it. Encouragement is your way of noticing when something is right – and putting courage in them to continue in His path. Don't fall into either extreme of only using God's Word as a form of correction that is void of encouragement or merely using it for encouragement without correction. Both are needed.

"with great patience and instruction:" Be mindful *how* you teach and *what* you teach. Just as God is patient with you, prioritize being patient with others. For me, my impatience often comes out the quickest in the moments when I have to repeat myself. But when it comes to sharing God's truth, being ready to minister at all times, and being willing to correct gently, to correct strongly and to encourage – it will all require a great deal of repetition. Paul repeated himself so much throughout his letters and in his preaching, and here's what he had to say about it: *"Finally, my brothers, rejoice in the Lord. To write the same things to you is no trouble to me and is safe for you"* (Philippians 3:1). Beyond Paul's patience, look at the result – the foundation of God's Word is safety. The further we stray from it, the more damage we can do to ourselves and to others. Repeat His truth to yourself and others with patience and joy.

4:3   Paul is warning Timothy about the progression of what will come concerning false teachers. Warning others about what they will encounter in a broken world as they live for Christ, is part of how we equip them. Transparently, warning is certainly not the most fun part, but it's necessary. As you disciple others, warn them as specifically as you can about what it may look like or feel like when they encounter certain situations. The particular circumstance Paul warned Timothy about still exists today. It is difficult to teach what most don't want to hear. Especially since technology like social media makes it so easy to measure who *likes* what you have to say and how many are paying attention. Please remember this: faithfulness is not a popularity contest. The gauge for the effectiveness of teaching has nothing to do with audience size or the world's approval rating. Plainly put, **effective teaching sounds like God.** And this means matching the character of God and the truth of His Word, not simply having charisma. That is what matters. His Word always accomplishes what He pleases and never returns void *(Isaiah 55:11)*. Paul says it himself right here – commitment to sound doctrine is a matter of endurance. And those who will not endure it desire to hear what they *want* to hear, not what they *need* to hear. They want teachers that justify their feelings and desires that align with the flesh...and they're not hard to find. Paul knew there would be enough of these teachers so those who desire them could *"accumulate"* them. Don't be surprised when you're the minority. Just remember that God's side, even if it appears to be outnumbered, will never be overpowered.

4:4   Myths are no different now than they were then. In opposition to truth, myths are made-up beliefs to justify sin. Myths result from taking Scripture out of context, dismissing Scripture altogether, adding to Scripture or clinging to a half-truth instead of the full truth. This is one of the reasons why it's so important that we know God's Word for ourselves – so we can recognize when it has been altered or omitted. But also – if you are in Christ, the Holy Spirit dwells within you. And there is no such thing as half Holy Spirit or Holy Spirit Jr. My pastor, Bruce Frank, puts it this way: "It's not a matter of how much of the Holy Spirit you have – but *how much of you* the Holy Spirit has." Ask God for His discernment to help you identify myths. If you're not sure if something is right, go to God's Word for answers. God is not a God of confusion *(1 Corinthians 14:33)*. Notice that Paul says that those who turn to myths also turn away from the truth. Keep turning to the truth, and you won't fall for myths.

4:5 The *"but you"* is a reminder that Timothy is on a different path than the false teachers and their crowds. So instead of being like them, Paul encourages Timothy to:

"be sober in all things:" Remain calm. Think. Don't react quickly. Ask instead of assuming. Don't offer your opinion on things that don't concern you. Refuse to make a big deal out of something that's really not a big deal. Don't fly off the handle over a news headline. Restrain yourself and be reasonable. All of these things may seem like common sense, but you've likely observed this for yourself: common *sense* does not mean common *practice*. We live in a world that is quick to react – and react *publicly*. (Yes, social media counts as public!) We're quick to judge, quick to be offended, quick to get angry and quick to divide over minor issues. But as believers, we're held to a different standard. We're called to be *"quick to listen, slow to speak and slow to become angry" (James 1:19)*. We're called to pursue peace *(Romans 14:19)*. We're not just called to consider if something is permissible – but if it's beneficial *(1 Corinthians 10:23)*. Slow down your reactions so you have time to pray and respond in a way that demonstrates how God calls us to live – *"in all things"* – not just the moments that are easier to be sober in, but the difficult ones too.

"endure hardship:" Endurance isn't required for easy. For example, you need endurance to be able to run three miles – but not so much to chill on the couch all day. Living for Christ requires our effort and guarantees that we will encounter hardship. We will continually have to tap into endurance. [Review the commentary note on 2 Timothy 3:11-12 for more on hardship – specifically, persecution and suffering.] But let me encourage you with this: hardship and joy can co-exist – if you keep your eyes on Jesus. If you focus on your hardship, finding joy will be hard. Not to mention, walking around, displaying your hardship like a badge of misery, doesn't encourage anyone to take steps closer to Christ. In 2 Corinthians 2:14-15, Paul wrote that, *"through us, [God] spreads the fragrance of the knowledge of*

Him everywhere." So as lovingly as I can say it – don't stink. The *"aroma of Christ"* is one that should make people want to linger a little longer, breathe in a little deeper, and create curiosity for what we have in Christ. Endure hardship – and do it with joy by keeping your eyes on Jesus.

"do the work of an evangelist:" Evangelism is a fancy church word for telling others about Jesus. Some have the gift of evangelism for sure. But the call to evangelize – to tell others about Christ – is not merely reserved for those with the gift of evangelism. We are all called to make disciples *(Matthew 28:19-20)*. Here's a new way to look at this: as you go about your life, remember the lost. Remember what your life was like before you knew Christ. Look for others who are spiritually where you used to be. Alone, you cannot tell everyone about Jesus, but everyone can tell someone about Jesus. One of my friends and pastors, Jason Gaston, has been asking one question for years now, and it has been so fun to see it take off in various circles of believers. The question is simply: *"Who's your one?"* Your one, being defined as someone who is close to you but far from Christ. So...who's *your* one? Be intentional to spend time with them. Ask them questions, and really listen to them. Pray for them, and pray with them. Love them really well. Encourage them with truth from God's Word. Tell them how much God loves them and what Jesus has done for them. *That* is doing the work of an evangelist.

"fulfill your ministry:" Ministry is not merely the work that is done inside churches and non-profit organizations. Ministry is anything a believer does that is submitted to God for Him to use. Timothy's ministry was pastoring the people in Ephesus. What's the ministry God has called you to fulfill? Don't overthink this – it may not have a title. Maybe you feel like God has called you to several places right now. Or maybe you feel the place God has called you is primarily inside your home. Whatever ministry He has given you to do, stay the course. Don't quit. Don't get distracted. Finish what God has started. The letters Paul wrote were shared between churches and as we know, many of his letters ended up being included in the New Testament. But when a letter from Paul first arrived, it would have been read aloud to the entire church. At the end of his letter to Collosae, Paul wrote, *"And say to Archippus, "See that you fulfill the ministry that you have received in the Lord"* (Colossians 4:17). Can you imagine being Archippus when that was read aloud in front of everyone? But I bet it worked! I'd say that was sufficient motivation to fulfill the ministry God had given him. I pray this can be your moment too.

_____, **fufill your ministry.**

[YOUR NAME HERE]

It matters. Together, as believers, we make up the body of Christ. The whole body benefits if you do your part, and the whole body suffers if you do not. [Read 1 Corinthians 12 to go deeper on this.] God has given you a ministry. Fulfill it.

4:6   The language Paul uses here is so powerful because a *"drink offering"* was Old Testament language that implies his death will be a sacrifice for the gospel. But this is my favorite part: Paul doesn't say he is pouring himself out, but that he is being *"poured out."* Paul acknowledges that God is in full control. Just as he has trusted God with his life, Paul trusts Him with his death. Because of his hope in Jesus, Paul has been at peace with death for a while now. In his letter to the church at Philippi, he wrote, *"I am hard pressed between the two [life and death]. My desire is to depart and be with Christ, for that is far better. But to remain in the flesh is more necessary on your account. Convinced of this, I know that I will remain and continue with you all, for your progress and joy in the faith, so that in me you may have ample cause to glory in Christ Jesus, because of my coming to you again" (Philippians 1:23-26).* At that time, Paul was convinced that even though he was prepared to die, he could be used for the gospel more if he were alive. Here, we see him having the same confidence in the gospel for his upcoming death. A reminder for us: If you are living in the power of Christ, God will pour you out. And Him pouring you out will be so much more powerful than the best performance you could muster up on your own. Paul was awesome, but he was still just a man. The perspective he shows here is evidence of Christ at work. A mere man in his own power doesn't sit in a jail cell, awaiting his execution, calmly referring to his death as a *"departure."* To make the greatest gospel difference, let God pour into you and let God pour you out.

4:7   No one would have predicted this would be how Paul would finish because his life is drastically different from how he started. Paul persecuted Christians. He made it his personal mission to put an end to Christianity. He was too young at the time to participate in the martyring of Stephen, but he was enough of an up and coming leader among the Pharisees that he was in charge of holding the robes of the men who stoned Stephen. [You can read the account in Acts 7:58-Acts 8:3.] Holding the robes may not sound like that big of a deal, but think about why the men took their robes off. Have you ever seen a baseball player wear heavy clothes? Of course not. Baseball uniforms are form fitting and lightweight, so they can have maximum power when they throw the ball. And that was Paul's *(known at the time as Saul)* job: to hold the robes so that the men could produce maximum pain every time they threw a stone. But praise God, the gospel doesn't take into account how we start. The gospel is about what Jesus finished for us on the cross and with His resurrection. Despite how Paul started, he finished with Jesus. And by the grace of God, the same is possible for each of us too. No matter your past, no matter the sins you've committed, no matter how you started – you can finish with Jesus.

"I have fought the good fight:" Only fight the good fight – the one of truth. Don't get distracted by inferior fights – let those go.

"I have finished the course:" Do what Jesus asks of you. No more. No less. He is the finish line.

"I have kept the faith:" Don't stop believing. *(And if you sang that in the style of Journey, you're my people.)* Keep coming back to your faith in what Christ has done and what He will do.

4:8 We often talk about how God will judge in eternity – but God will also reward. The reason why reward talk gets tricky is probably out of fear of not wanting to get swept up in the prosperity gospel. The prosperity gospel *is* a false gospel that preaches that the better you behave, the more God will reward you. Essentially, if you're rich and healthy, God is pleased with you. But if you're sick or poor, you must have done something to offend God. There is no Biblical basis for the prosperity gospel whatsoever. But we do need to remember, like Paul does here, that one day – not here on this earth – but one day, in Heaven, God will reward those who believed. Paul's moment of receiving God's reward is close, but here, he reminds us that this reward is available to all who believe – not merely for him because he started a lot of churches or wrote most of the New Testament. God is not after your performance, but your faithful finish. Heaven doesn't give out gold, silver and bronze medals – everyone who finishes faithfully gets a crown of righteousness that Jesus earned for us. Eternity is real. Standing before God is real. And His reward is real too.

2 Timothy 4:1-8

QUESTIONS

Icebreaker: What do you think about participation trophies? Do you love them, or are you annoyed by them? Are they ever appropriate, or should there always be a winner and a loser?

1. As his mentor, Paul had some authority over Timothy -- but when it came time to challenge him, Paul pointed to God's position in Timothy's life -- not his own. Practically, what are some ways you can point to God's authority in the lives of those you have influence over instead of your own?

2. In 2 Timothy 4:2, Paul charges Timothy to *"be ready in season and out of season."* This means to be consistently willing to minister in all moments -- not merely when it's comfortable, convenient or conventional. What is one of your *"in season"* circumstances when you feel comfortable ministering and one of your *"out of season"* situations where the idea of ministering seems more intimidating?

3. Discuss the differences between what it means to *"reprove, rebuke and exhort"* (2 Timothy 4:2). Of the three, which one do you feel you put into practice the least often? Why?

4. Read 2 Timothy 4:3-4. What are your biggest concerns about false teachers? What makes false teachers attractive? How do we protect ourselves from falling for a false gospel?

5. 2 Timothy 4:5 reminds us to *"be sober in all things."* In your own words, describe what this means. Go around the group and share one way you need to be held accountable to live this out.

6. Discuss what it means to *"do the work of an evangelist"* (2 Timothy 4:5). Who's your one? Share with the group, and pray for each other.

7. Paul was ready to die because he knew he had fulfilled his ministry. Despite how he started, that's why near the end, he could say: *"I have fought the good fight, I have finished the course, I have kept the faith"* (2 Timothy 4:7). What are some things you need to remember so at the end of your life, you can do the same?

2 Timothy 4:9-22

COMMENTARY

4:9-22   Paul saved his personal matters for last. The reminders of the gospel, dwelling on the goodness of God and the hope of heaven, and both his encouragement and warning for Timothy – those were the things that were pressing on Paul's heart to write first. As we will learn more in detail from these verses, Paul's current situation is far from favorable: he's cold, he's lonely, and recently, he was left alone to defend himself in court. But despite the difficulty, his circumstances were not at the forefront of his mind: Jesus was. While we don't typically rush toward them, hard times often provide us with the clearest perspective. When things are good or even just easy, we can be quick to fall into an *"I got this"* mentality. With that mindset, the smallest inconveniences can drive us to endless cycles of complaining and entitlement. Though Paul has real reasons to complain, because he is fully reliant on the Lord, his personal concerns are not his top concern. Pay attention when you find yourself drawn to dwell on your circumstances instead of setting your mind on God and others. You can't always change your circumstance, but you can always change your perspective.

4:9-12   Paul was lonely. During this imprisonment, the few people who have been with him are no longer there. These verses share where they've gone: *Demas* left for Thessalonica, *"having loved this present world" (vs. 10)*. There is a difference between loving the world for what it has to offer us and loving the people who occupy the world. Aim to love the people in the world as you refuse to give your affections to what the world offers you. Demas loved the things of the world so much that he left his ministry to pursue more of the world. The same would easily be true for any of us. Getting caught up in what this world has to offer you limits your ability to live for Christ. As for *Crecens*, *Titus* and *Tychicus*, Paul sent them to meet the needs of the people at the churches they had started on their missionary journeys. Paul put the needs of others above his own needs. You will always be aware of your own needs, but like it says in Philippians 2:3-4, we are to count others as more significant than ourselves and not merely look to our own interests, but to the interests of others. Open your eyes to see beyond your own needs so you can meet the needs of others. See separate note on 4:11 for more on Mark.

4:11 This is one of my favorite verses of 2 Timothy. Paul and Mark have a long history. When Paul went on his first missionary journey with Barnabas, Mark went with them. We don't know what happened exactly, but halfway through their trip, Mark left to go home to Jerusalem *(Acts 13:13)*. When it was time for their second missionary journey, Barnabas wanted to bring Mark with them again. You can read the whole account in Acts 15:36-41, but Paul and Barnabas, who had been an unstoppable gospel force together for many years, disagreed so strongly over whether Mark should go with them or not that they ended up going separate ways. Paul took Silas with him, and Barnabas took Mark with him. This verse is the only hint of the rest of the story. We don't know how they reconciled, but this verse lets us know that they did. Paul used to question Mark's commitment, but now, he regards him as useful in his ministry. Again, we don't know the details of the specific circumstances that caused Mark to leave in the middle of their first missionary journey. But this verse reminds us that God can change people. No person or relationship is too far gone for God to be able to reach. [If you have never studied the book of Acts, check out our *Conversational Commentary on Acts: The Gospel Mission Then and Now*.]

4:13 In addition to being lonely, Paul was cold. He wants his coat before winter. But take a step back and examine what Paul has shared he longs for: basic needs *(a coat)*, God's people *(he wants Timothy and Mark to come visit him)*, and *"the parchments"* - so Paul could continue to minister while in prison. *Parchments* could have referred to the Old Testament or they could have referred to thick, quality paper so he could continue writing letters to people and churches. Paul is not trying to escape his circumstances. What he asks for is the bare minimum for what will help him keep ministering to the very end. When you are in difficult situations, turn to God's Word, turn to God's people, and continue your ministry.

4:14-15 This could be someone new, or this could be the Alexander he wrote to Timothy about in his first letter. [See 1 Timothy 1:20.] As you go about your life, just as Alexander wronged Paul, you can expect to be wronged too. Paul has two basic responses: First, he trusts God to bring justice. Paul would have been justified to want to bring about justice for himself, but he chose to remember that justice is God's job. Have peace when you are wronged and know that one day, every wrong will be made right – but it's not your job to make it happen. God will bring justice. Second, while Paul did not seek revenge on Alexander, he did feel responsibility to warn Timothy about him. Remember, though, this is a private letter. Paul choosing to warn Timothy about Alexander is not condoning gossip or public condemnation.

4:16   When Paul stood on trial, no one came with him. But instead of blaming them, Paul forgave them. Paul knows his death is coming. When the finality of your earthly life is coming quickly, I'd assume it's much easier to distinguish between major and minor offenses. But in the heat of the moment, no offense *feels* minor. A mentor once told me, "Don't spend five minutes being angry over what you won't remember in five years." Aim to forgive rather than blame. Yes, people are hard. Ministry is hard. But bitterness adds a whole new level of difficulty, while forgiveness frees you from it. Remember, we're not just supposed to forgive when it's easy or when it makes sense. We are to forgive as we have been forgiven *(Ephesians 4:32)*.

4:17   Because of God, Paul knew he wasn't alone in court. God was with him. God promises that He will never leave us or forsake us *(Deuteronomy 31:8)*. In the moments when you're alone and desire companionship, remind yourself that God is standing with you. He will strengthen you. He will work through you and speak through you. In an earlier letter to the church at Corinth, Paul wrote that God's power *"is made perfect in weakness"* (2 Corinthians 12:9). In the moments when you know you need to be at your best, pray that you will show up in weakness – so God's power will be made perfect. When you rely on your own strength, you are limited. Paul's weakness allowed for his testimony to be fully given, for all the Gentiles to hear, and for God to rescue Paul from being executed then. Show up weak and be confident God can strengthen you.

4:18   No matter what happens to him on earth, salvation is Paul's rescue. Because of Jesus, death does not prevail or get the final say. Heaven is our rescue from *"every evil deed,"* and God is our Rescuer. Though he will be executed, Paul knows God will bring him *"safely to His heavenly kingdom."* What happens to you in your earthly life is not the end. For those who are in Christ, we are rescued and brought safely to heaven. It's nothing we could earn or do in our own power. God gets every bit of the glory.

4:19-21   Paul's last letter is no different from the many he has written before. He ends by showing his love for people – the people who are with him and the people who are with Timothy. We live in a world where it's easy to live in isolation. Because of technology, we can even be isolated while claiming to be connected. The flesh is often drawn to the mountaintop moments, the important tasks and the exciting positions – and none of that is necessarily bad in and of itself. For example, when you and I think about the scope of Paul's ministry, we probably see it through the lens of his accomplishments, such as the cities where he planted churches. But as Paul displays here, he saw faces. Ministry is so much better defined in names and faces than by stages and achievements. It's a beautiful thing to desire to be part of God's work in the world. But instead of asking God for something to do, ask Him for someone to serve. *That* is ministry.

4:22   Paul remained in awe of God's grace until the very end, and we must too. For a faithful finish, you don't need a different set of circumstances, a new skill set, an easier path, a better resumé, a larger crowd, or a controlled outcome. You need grace – God's grace for you, which you can then extend to others.

2 Timothy 4:9-22

QUESTIONS

Icebreaker: What one-sentence piece of advice would you give to the person who is a decade behind you?

1. Paul waits until the very end of his letter to address his personal concerns. What does that prove about his priorities? What are some practical ways that we can identify if our priorities are where they should be or if they are misplaced?

2. In 2 Timothy 4:10, Paul tells Timothy that Demas left him because he *"loved this present world."* Getting caught up in what the world had to offer him limited his willingness to live for Christ. What do you think are some of the things the world offers that are easy to get caught up in? Practically, what does it look like to live in the world and love the people around us without loving what the world has to offer us?

3. In 2 Timothy 4:9-13, Paul lists four things he wants: for Timothy to make every effort to come visit him soon, to bring Mark with him, to bring him his coat, and to bring him books/parchments. Remember that Paul is in prison, awaiting execution. What can we learn from what Paul asks for *and* what he doesn't ask for?

4. Even though Paul was wronged by Alexander the coppersmith, Paul refuses to seek justice against him *(2 Timothy 4:14)*. We see a similar spirit of forgiveness when Paul shares that no one came to be with him when he had to give his defense in court *(2 Timothy 4:16)*. How much more energy do you think we would have for Kingdom work if we refused to seek revenge or harbor unforgiveness? How do you remind yourself to forgive others as you have been forgiven?

5. Read 2 Timothy 4:17-18. When you read these verses, what truths stand out to you that you need to cling to now? What reminders does this give us for our future in heaven?

6. Paul concludes his letter the way he usually did with many personal greetings. The world we live in today not only bends toward making

isolation easy, but it also tends to only offer praise for the work that is done for the masses. Why is that mindset in complete opposition to the charge to *"fulfill your ministry?"* How can we shift our desire from wanting to do something for God to desiring to serve someone with God?

7. In his final words, Paul encourages Timothy to lean on grace. In your own words, what is grace? Why is it what we need? What does it look like to live a life that is fueled by grace? In the absence of being fueled by grace, what sources would we turn to instead? Why would those sources never be able to accomplish what grace can accomplish?

Recommended Books & Resources

FOR DEEPER STUDY

―――――――――――

Strong's Exhaustive Concordance of the Bible

Strong, James. *The New Strong's Exhaustive Concordance of the Bible : With Main Concordance, Appendix to the Main Concordance, Hebrew and Aramaic Dictionary of the Old Testament, Greek Dictionary of the New Testament.* Nashville Tenn., T. Nelson, 1997.

The Expositor's Bible Commentary 1 and 2 Thessalonians, 1 and 2 Timothy, Titus

Tremper Longman, Iii, and David E Garland. *The Expositor's Bible Commentary 1 and 2 Thessalonians, 1 and 2 Timothy, Titus.* Grand Rapids, Mich., Zondervan, 2017.

Christ-Centered Exposition Series

Platt, D., Akin, D. L., & Merida, T. (2013). *Exalting Jesus in 1 & 2 Timothy and Titus.* B & H Academic.

The ESV Study Bible

Crossway Bibles. *ESV : Study Bible : English Standard Version.* Wheaton, Ill., Crossway Bibles, 2016.

Systematic Theology by Wayne Grudem

Grudem, Wayne A. *Systematic Theology.* Grand Rapids, Mich., Zondervan, 1994.

The Visual Word by Patrick Schreiner

Schreiner, Patrick, and Anthony M. Benedetto. *The Visual Word: Illustrated Outlines of the New Testament Books.* Chicago, Moody Publishers, 2021.

The Bible Project

Book of 2 Timothy summary: Watch an overview video. BibleProject. (n.d.). https://bibleproject.com/explore/video/2-timothy/

ESV Story of Redemption Bible

Not Available. *HOLY BIBLE : English Standard Version, Story of Redemption Bible.* Crossway, 2018.

Pocket Dictionary of Theological Terms (Grenz, Guretzki + Nordling)
Grenz, Stanley J, et al. *Pocket Dictionary of Theological Terms.* Downers Grove, Ill., Intervarsity Press, 1999.

Dictionary of Paul and His Letters
Hawthorne, Gerald F., et al. *Dictionary of Paul and His Letters a Compendium of Contemporary Biblical Scholarship.* InterVarsity Press, 2015.

SWHW
SHE WORKS HIS WAY

A discipleship community for working women who love Jesus.

If you've been looking for a community to come alongside you as you navigate the tension between what God's Word says and what culture wants us to believe, you belong here!

JOIN THE SWHW NETWORK:
SHEWORKSHISWAY.COM

We just know and believe in the power of gathering women together who want their work (inside & outside the home) to matter for the Kingdom of God. If you've been craving community, but don't know where to start — can we encourage you to start here? This simple step — choosing to invest in and equip yourself — can have an eternal impact on you, your people and your community. We'd love nothing more than to have you join the party!

THE SWHW PODCAST

You're invited into a conversation about how to navigate the tension between what God says and what culture wants you to believe, both Biblically and practically.

NEW EPISODE EVERY MONDAY

THE
SHE WORKS HIS WAY
PODCAST

NEW EPISODE EVERY MONDAY

Scan code to connect with us

ADDITIONAL RESOURCES FROM SWHW:

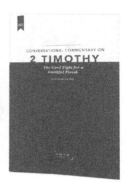

CONVERSATIONAL COMMENTARIES SERIES

SWHW BOOK + STUDY GUIDE, FAMOUS IN HEAVEN & AT HOME

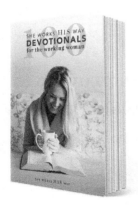

100 DAILY DEVOTIONALS FOR THE WORKING WOMAN VOLS 1, 2, +3

SHEWORKSHISWAY.COM/SHOP

Become a
SHE WORKS HIS WAY
DONOR

100% of your gift helps us provide discipleship training for women and local churches around the world.

SHE WORKS HIS WAY is a registered 501(c)(3) non-profit organization.

SHEWORKSHISWAY.COM/DONATE

Made in the USA
Coppell, TX
08 August 2023

20134223R00049